SUCK LESS, LAUGH MORE

A FOUR-PART FORMULA FOR BEING A GREAT DAD

Brian Gray

PUBLISHED BY AVOCET BOOKS
www.avocetbooks.com

Hardcover 978-1-963678-12-3
Softcover 978-1-963678-11-6
eBook 978-1-963678-13-0

First Edition

BOOK PRODUCTION BY AVOCET BOOKS
www.avocetbooks.com

Suck Less, Laugh More

CONTENTS

Dedication

To my wonderful wife, Vika. Thank you.

*To my two daughters, Leah and Eva. You two
have made me want to be a better human,
which has ripple effects in all aspects of my life.*

*To my good friend, Dave Moszkiewicz,
who I wish could read this book.*

Introduction

Am I a successful dad?
Am I guiding my kids the right way?
Am I a good role model?

As a father raising kids in our modern world, these questions used to cross my mind a lot—and boy, were they stressful. I mean, it is easier to figure out a Rubik's Cube blindfolded than to figure out modern parenting.

If you've picked up this book, you've likely had similar questions cross your mind. Raising a family is hard these days. There's a lot to navigate between expectations, financial obligations, and teaching our kin how to succeed in a fast-paced and ever-changing environment.

Moreover, we've been heavily programmed.

From an early age, we are programmed to think we need to strive for success. In our culture, success is celebrated, and if we aren't successful, our life becomes an uphill battle, fraught with financial stress, unfulfilled dreams, and missed opportunities.

In other words, our lives will suck.

So, we follow the script given to us: get good grades, graduate college, find a job that pays the bills, find a partner to marry, buy a house, have children, make more money, buy more things, and so on.

We're programmed to think this script will make us happy, that our lives will be fulfilled, and that somehow this will spill over into fatherhood and make us good fathers.

But does it?

It certainly didn't for me. Instead, it only complicated things and drove me to get drunk. Despite following the script into my forties, my life was still an uphill battle in more ways than one.

As you will soon find out in the pages that follow, I launched myself on a wildly fulfilling journey in breaking up my programming. After seeing improvements in every corner of my life, I now want to help others—especially dads like you—navigate our modern world in a way that is more peaceful, satisfying, and fun.

In short, to suck less and laugh more.

During my quest, I tried searching for answers online and via outside help, and through books, podcasts, and mentorship. While these were honorable endeavors, they often left me overwhelmed.

Perhaps you've had a similar experience.

I wrote this book to help other dads avoid that. Truth be told, being a good dad is quite simple. At its root, it means being principled and ethical throughout our lives. Dads should be kings of their kingdom. When you've mastered what you *truly* want and what you *truly* stand for, you are a better son, a better husband, a better colleague, a better neighbor, and better leader for your family and your kingdom.

But being a good king is only one part of the equation.

Sucking less and laughing more is rooted in understanding the four archetypes within us. Just like there are four seasons in a year, four cardinal directions (north, south, east, west), and four sides to a square, each of us has four internal archetypes we need to acknowledge and honor.

I refer to these archetypes as the Four Parts of a Superior Dad.

And the best part is that you already have each one within you.

The Four Parts:
Understanding Your Inner Framework

You have four archetypes within you—the Warrior, the King, the Wizard, and the Jester—and together, they form a framework for understanding yourself and how you engage with the world. Each one represents a distinct part of your inner self, offering unique strengths and insights to help you navigate life's challenges, relationships, and ambitions. By getting to know these archetypes, you'll uncover powerful tools to grow, connect, and thrive. They're not just characters—they're parts of you, waiting to be understood and empowered.

Each archetype needs the right kind of fuel to thrive—what I like to call "jet fuel." Why jet fuel? Because you're not just any machine—you're a high-performance being, built for extraordinary things. Just like a jet engine can't run on regular gas, you need a specific kind of fuel to reach your full potential. I like to use the image of jet fuel because you have to be intentional about what you're fueling yourself with. This isn't about pulling into the nearest gas station and hoping for the best. It's about thoughtfully choosing the kind of fuel that truly powers you forward. Without the right jet fuel, your archetypes will find ways to get their needs met in less-than-ideal ways—like procrastination, stress-eating, or endlessly scrolling TikTok.

But when you give yourself the right jet fuel, you unlock the power to operate at your best. It's the key to breaking free from unproductive habits and shifting into a higher gear—one that fuels growth, fulfillment, and purpose.

Each chapter dives into one archetype: who they are, what they need, and how to keep them thriving (their jet fuel). Along the way, I'll share stories of how these archetypes have shown up in my life—sometimes hilariously, sometimes painfully—and how I learned to give them what they actually needed.

The journey begins with awareness of your archetypes and ends with empowerment—knowing how to nurture each part of yourself. The goal is to help you identify these patterns and replace them with empowering strategies.

Chapter 1 explores your **Inner Warrior**, who craves certainty and structure. This is your go-getter, your action-taker. But don't let him get too comfortable, or he'll settle for mediocrity. The Warrior's jet fuel? A crystal-clear vision. When you know exactly what you're working toward, the Warrior gets fired up and unstoppable.

Chapter 2 is dedicated to your **Inner Wizard**, your emotional compass. He craves connection—both with others and with yourself. Without his jet fuel, however, the Wizard can get lost in distractions like endless news cycles or social media. His jet fuel? Emotional mastery. When you learn to navigate your emotions, the Wizard transforms into a guide for deeper relationships and self-awareness.

Chapter 3 dives into your **Inner King**, who is all about significance and purpose. He wants to feel important—but in the right way. Without the proper fuel, he'll chase drama or sit around moaning about problems to feel validated. The King's jet fuel? Living your values. When you align your actions with what really matters, your King steps up to lead with integrity.

And lastly, chapter 4 expands on your **Inner Jester**, your inner child, your spark of curiosity, and your appetite for adventure. Ignore it, and he'll seek variety in not-so-healthy ways—like binge-watching Netflix or pouring one too many glasses of whiskey. The Jester's jet fuel? Humor and playfulness. He thrives on trying new things, taking risks, and laughing at the inevitable stumbles along the way.

The Path to Growth Is Your Choice

Getting to know these archetypes opens up a choice: Will you nurture them in ways that push you forward, or will you let them hold you back? Too often, we meet their needs in ways that hold us back.

For example, your Warrior might get stuck playing it safe, clinging to what's comfortable instead of chasing what's possible. Your Wizard might search for connection by doom scrolling, bingeing on distractions, or numbing emotions instead of addressing them. Your King might stay busy solving everyone's problems but never actually live his own purpose. Your Jester might seek variety at the bottom of a bottle of wine instead of embracing meaningful change.

Sound familiar? Yeah, me too. Been there, done that. These disempowering strategies are like junk food for your archetypes. They might satisfy you for a moment, but they leave you feeling worse in the long run.

This book is about swapping the junk food for real nourishment. When you give your archetypes the proper jet fuel, they stop working against you and start pulling you forward. Your Warrior will rise to meet challenges with purpose. Your Wizard will create meaningful connections. Your King will lead with clarity and confidence. And your Jester will turn fear of failure into curiosity and laughter.

The beauty of this framework is that it is easy to remember and even easier to apply. Understanding the Four Parts of a Superior Dad makes life better. When you know how to nurture each archetype, you'll break free from those same old cycles that leave you feeling stuck. Instead of defaulting to disempowering ways of meeting your needs, you can ask yourself, *What's a better way to satisfy this part of me?* That's where the real growth happens—when you consciously feed these archetypes in ways that align with your values and create a meaningful, lasting impact.

By the end of this book, you'll know how to balance all four archetypes and feed them in ways that build the life you actually want.

The Interwoven Journey of Growth

This book introduces the archetypes in the order I discovered them in my own life, but that doesn't mean your journey will follow the same path. The archetypes aren't a step-by-step process—they're a dynamic, overlapping cycle. Each one influences the others, and together they create a powerful framework for growth.

You don't need to start with one and master it before moving on. Maybe you're drawn to your Inner Wizard first, working on mastering your emotions, and along the way, your Inner Jester emerges, laughing at the stumbles you make. Or perhaps your Inner King calls to you, guiding you to align with your values, even as your Warrior steps in to keep your vision on track. The beauty of this framework is its flexibility—you get to decide where to begin and what feels most important to you right now.

These archetypes aren't separate; they work together. For the sake of clarity, this book explores them one at a time, but in practice, they're constantly overlapping and interacting. Wherever you choose to start, know this: this journey never truly ends. The more aware you become of your archetypes, the more you can make empowering decisions—and with each choice, the cycle through the archetypes begins anew, unlocking deeper growth and transformation.

After this book, you'll understand that making progress toward your vision, like a Warrior with a clear mission, is a form of happiness.

You'll tap into your Wizard to master your emotions, your King to live with purpose and values, and your Jester to embrace playfulness—creating a sense of optimism by laughing at yourself a little more, and sucking a little less.

A Bit About Me

When I first recognized these archetypes in myself, everything changed. It was a game-changer. Suddenly, I could see how some parts of me were working against the life I wanted. For instance, my need for variety? Let's just say I was meeting it in ways that weren't exactly healthy. We all fall into that trap from time to time.

As I reflected on how these archetypes showed up in my own life, I realized my Inner Warrior had been running the show since high school. And not just running it—dominating it.

Let me take you back. According to my driver's license at sixteen, I was 5'0" tall and weighed 95 pounds. Sounds small, right? Except it was a lie. The truth? I was 4'11" and weighed 89 pounds soaking wet.

I was the runt of my class, and when you're the runt, you get picked on—a lot. I was bullied in middle school and high school, and it was common (and easy) for bigger classmates to pick me up and throw me into trash cans.

Back then, there wasn't much to do about bullying. You certainly didn't tell anyone—not your teachers, not your parents, not even your friends. Doing so would have just guaranteed a few more trips to the trash can.

But those experiences awakened something in me: my Inner Warrior. And boy, did he show up with a vengeance. My Warrior became a cut-throat achiever, determined to prove to the world that I wasn't just some small, insignificant kid. I wanted to prove that I was a giant—a King. At the time, I thought the only path to being a King was through the Warrior. So I worked harder than anyone, achieved more than anyone, and made sure no one underestimated me.

And for the most part, I succeeded.

I developed a formula for success:

If I don't succeed, I will not have money.

If I don't have money, I'll be miserable.

Which naturally led to its antithesis:

If I am successful and have money, I'll be happy.

And—wow—did my Warrior love this formula. I was all in.

In school, I got good grades. After high school, I pursued a career in finance. I graduated college, landed a good job, passed the CPA exam, married my beautiful wife, bought a house, became a father, and eventually made partner at my CPA firm. By the time I was a partner, I was making a quarter million per year.

On paper, I was ultra-successful. I had everything anyone could dream of. Hell, I even surpassed my own expectations at times. From the outside, people saw me as a King.

But inside, I certainly didn't feel like one.

After seventeen years of relentlessly following this success script, I was exhausted. None of it brought true happiness. If anything, it pushed me toward alcohol. I became a binge drinker, drifting further away from my wife and kids. My success formula wasn't working.

Why wasn't I happy?

The obvious answer was that I wasn't fulfilled. I had pinned all my hopes on the belief that happiness would magically appear once I reached the next milestone. But each time I achieved a goal—whether it was graduating college, buying my first house, or becoming a partner—it left me feeling hollow. Accomplishments didn't bring the joy I thought they would.

But the less obvious answer? I was stuck in my Inner Warrior.

The Warrior had run the show for so long that the other archetypes never had a chance. And while my Warrior was great at conquering visions, he had a one-track mind. My relationships were surface-level. My health wasn't great. My role as a husband was . . . let's just say, not award-winning. I had zero balance in my life.

And every time I hit a goal, I sabotaged myself by drinking.

I knew about the King archetype—hell, I wanted to be the King. But I had no idea how to bring him out in a positive way. The King is rooted in our need for significance. We all have that need. The question is: Do you tear others down to feel significant, or do you build others up, which in turn elevates you?

For me, the missing link was my Inner Wizard. No one ever told me about the Wizard (or the Jester, for that matter). It wasn't until I began mastering my emotions through the Wizard that I started to find fulfillment. That's when everything started to shift.

To truly bring balance into my life, I had to get in touch with the archetypes I'd been neglecting. That's what this book is about—the journey of discovering and nurturing the four archetypes that make us whole.

For me, exploring these archetypes has been transformative. It's improved my mental wellness, deepened my relationships, and brought me a sense of fulfillment I never thought possible. Honestly, it's helped me grow up—finally—in my late forties.

And here's the good news: it's never too late.

I went from being a passive passenger in life—letting it just happen to me—to becoming the conductor of my own symphony. Now I know what I want, when I want it, and how I want to get there. And let me tell you, it feels incredible.

I want the same for you.

Why I Wrote This Book

Humans have an innate desire to teach and help others. When we unlock a secret or discover something that improves our lives, the first thing we want to do is share it. We want our friends, family, and everyone we care about to feel that same sense of satisfaction, healing, or clarity.

That's why I wrote this book—to help other dads who might be struggling.

I also wanted to simplify the process. Let's be real—being a superior dad doesn't have to be overwhelming or complicated. During my journey, I stumbled upon *The Success Principles: How to Get from Where You Are to Where You Want to Be* by Jack Canfield. That book, published in 2006, was a game-changer for me. I learned a ton, even joined his mastermind group, and applied much of what I read. But there was just so much to it—maybe even too much. I wanted a version that was easier to digest and implement, something that felt more like a *Reader's Digest*.

And honestly? His book didn't speak to my people.

I wanted a book that speaks directly to dads in their late thirties and forties, dads who are navigating career, family, and personal growth all at once. That's the book I set out to write—the one you're holding in your hands right now.

But let me be clear: if you've picked up this book and you're not a dad, that's okay! This book is really about becoming the best version of yourself. If you're a mom, feel free to substitute "Inner King" with "Inner Queen." The principles here are universal, though I write from the perspective of a dad because that's my lane.

I wrote this book not only to help dads thrive at home but also to inspire us to rise up as confident, active members of our communities. When we're grounded in who we are and what we value, we can start standing up for the things we believe in—at the PTA meeting, in city hall, or even on a bigger stage. We need more dads who aren't afraid to step forward, run for office, and bring their best selves into the world.

But my biggest reason for writing this book?

Our kids.

As dads, we're in a unique and powerful position to shape the next generation. My goal is to lead my children in a way that makes their lives better than mine ever was. The world is a tough place, and it's not getting any easier. There's already too much division out there. What our kids need is unity, strength, and guidance—and that starts with us.

This book is a roadmap to becoming that kind of dad.

My hope is that it helps you gain some perspective. No matter what challenges you're facing, this is an incredible time to be alive. It's not the destination that matters; it's the person you're becoming along the way. And guess what? You're allowed to have fun during the process.

Each of the four archetypes—the Warrior, the King, the Wizard, and the Jester—is already within you, waiting to be nurtured and brought to life.

So if you're ready to step into your role as a superior dad, let's dive into chapter 1 and meet your Inner Warrior.

CHAPTER 1

Your Inner Warrior: Conquering Your Vision and Knowing Your Outcome

"Make the most of yourself for that is all there is of you."
—*Ralph Waldo Emerson*

You know that moment after a few drinks when you think, *"Oh shit, I'm drunk. I should stop?"*

Yeah, I didn't get those.

From the moment I entered the workforce, my Inner Warrior thrived. I poured massive amounts of energy, time, and effort into building a successful career, believing that success would bring me happiness. And when I reached a milestone, I wanted to celebrate. What better way to reward myself than with a drink—or two?

But I didn't stop with one celebratory drink.

I was a binge drinker.

I justified my drinking because of my accomplishments and the pressures of my role. As a CPA and partner in a public accounting firm with seventy-five employees, I carried a significant amount of responsibility. I helped highly successful entrepreneurs manage their tax liabilities—clients who paid millions in taxes every year. I'd worked incredibly hard to get to this point. If anyone deserved to let off some steam, it was 100 percent me.

And justifying it? That was easy. Most Americans drink—about 63 percent of adults, according to the CDC.[1] Social drinking is deeply woven into our culture, from happy hours and game nights to weddings and dinner parties. My parents were no exception. They drank to relax after a stressful day, to have fun, and to celebrate life—at dinner parties, football games, you name it. I grew up believing drinking equaled fun because it was everywhere. It wasn't just normal—it was expected.

I was programmed to think drinking equaled fun.

When I was growing up, my parents lived paycheck to paycheck. As a result, our vacations consisted of visiting places within driving distance, and upon arrival, drinking alcohol was the way my parents enjoyed themselves. As a young boy at home, I remember my dad enjoying a beer when he came home from work. In my family, alcohol

---

1   National Institute on Alcohol Abuse and Alcoholism, "Alcohol Facts and Statistics," updated 2022, accessed November 19, 2024, https://www.niaaa.nih.gov/alcohols-effects-health/alcohol-topics/alcohol-facts-and-statistics.

was a way of life. A few beers after work to relieve stress and more beer on the weekend to have fun was the norm.

Looking back, that's where the programming started.

I wasn't always a binge drinker, either. Like it does for most people, it crept up on me gradually. Between 2001 and 2012, I only drank occasionally—usually with colleagues or my wife over dinner. Excessive drinking was rare, happening maybe once or twice a year, typically after tax season. My team and I worked so hard; surely we deserved to celebrate!

But when I did let loose, I went apeshit.

When something happens once or twice a year, you can deal with it. But when it happens every other weekend? Well, that's a whole different story.

In our alcohol-saturated culture, finding drinking buddies was never a challenge—and I found plenty. My routine was simple: grind through the workday, then hit the bar to drink the night away. When the bars closed at 2 a.m., we'd move on to the only place still open—strip clubs. These escapades often had me stumbling home in the early hours of the morning, where my wife would be waiting, worried sick. She'd share her feelings—frustration, fear, and hurt—and I didn't want to hear a word of it.

One night in October 2017, I chose not to come home at all, avoiding my wife like a child avoiding punishment. I convinced myself it was easier to stay away than to face her and deal with the fallout.

"Hey, man—can I crash at your place tonight?" I asked my drinking buddy.

"Of course, dude!"

And just like that, I avoided going home—to my wife and two kids. I didn't want to ruin the high I was riding, and staying at his place meant we could keep the party going. In that moment, I acted like a carefree twenty-something bachelor, conveniently forgetting I was a forty-something married father.

Unsurprisingly, this brilliant avoidance strategy didn't work (shocker). Eventually, I had to face the music. Hungover and ashamed, I dragged myself home late Friday morning, the sun already high in the sky. As expected, my wife, Vika, was furious (because she had every right to be).

"You didn't come home last night," she said sternly.

"Yeah, I'm sorry," I responded, trying to get out of the discussion as fast as possible.

"Brian, this is not okay. I was worried about you. You didn't text, and when I tried calling you, it went straight to voicemail. Was your phone off?"

I didn't answer.

"This has to stop," she said, now more aggressively. "You are going to stop drinking or I am done."

Not thinking clearly, I grabbed some of my clothes and left the house for the nearby hotel. I was still hungover, and I was not sure what I wanted at that point. I felt pretty numb and indifferent.

In the car, I called my mom.

"Hey, Mom. Vika kicked me out . . . due to my drinking. No surprises there." Vika and I had previously been to marriage counseling regarding the same problem, so this wasn't exactly news to her.

"She says I need help," I continued. "Can you recommend a counselor, please?" My mom had been going to therapy for many years and had built a network of professionals. If anyone was to give a solid recommendation, it was Mom.

She gave me the number to Paul, a marriage and family therapist. After I checked into the hotel room, I rang his office and scheduled a session for the coming Monday.

That weekend, I happened to have a family event in Santa Barbara. I went alone. "Vika needed to stay home with the kids," I'd say to anyone who asked. No one needed to know the truth, and I was grateful to see family and keep myself occupied.

And guess what? I didn't drink.

Monday came around, and I met with my counselor. After explaining the situation, we talked for a bit, but he kept harping on one thing: "We need to get you back into the house." Paul repeated this phrase several times, and in retrospect, I appreciated this advice. I was so numb at the time. I didn't care what happened. I was ready to let go.

I didn't love the ultimatum from Vika (who would?). My ego was bruised and, still recovering from the alcohol, I had a "don't-give-a-fuck" attitude.

Deep down inside, however, I didn't want my marriage to end, and Paul must have sensed that.

"You gotta get back into the house, Brian. Do you think you can go today?"

"Maybe? But what about Vika?"

"Don't worry about her right now. Worry about yourself. You need to clean up your side of the street, and you need to go back home."

"She doesn't want me there, though. Shouldn't I respect her wishes? I need to get myself right."

"No, no, no," he said. "While, yes, you want to get better, and I appreciate that, we need to focus on this very moment. We need to focus on today. You are probably feeling pretty bad about yourself, which is totally normal, but we don't want to punish ourselves. Don't punish yourself any more than what you're feeling right now. You need to go home."

I appreciated his advice and listened. I got my stuff and left the hotel to return home. The energy between Vika and me was tense—stiff and cold. She needed more time, because of course she did. I understood. I needed to regain her trust and prove myself to her. Neither of which was going to happen overnight.

It was clear there was a gap in this part of my life, one I couldn't ignore any longer. I set a vision to close that gap and took the first steps by apologizing—sincerely. I apologized for my actions, for not coming home, for shutting her out and turning my phone off.

Then I made a promise: I told her I would quit drinking.

Meet Your Inner Warrior

Your Inner Warrior represents the part of you that craves certainty, structure, and stability. He's in all of us, whether we recognize it or not.

This archetype is responsible for fighting your battles—whether those battles are external challenges like work deadlines or internal struggles like self-doubt. The Warrior thrives on discipline, action, and having a clear mission. When it's working well, your Warrior gives you strength, focus, and the determination to persevere through tough times. It's the voice that says, *"I've got this,"* even when the odds might be stacked against you.

But here's the catch: when you're not properly fueling your Warrior, it can lead to stagnation or fear of the unknown. Maybe you've gotten too comfortable, settling into a routine that doesn't push you anymore. Or maybe you've let uncertainty paralyze you, leaving you stuck in place. A tired or unmotivated Warrior often clings to disempowering habits just to feel safe—like staying in a dead-end job, avoiding conflict, or over-planning without ever taking action.

Vision and clarity are power. To me, these two words go hand in hand; they're synonymous. When you have clarity—when you truly know your outcome—you unlock the ability to manifest anything. It's all connected. To create the life you want, you need to know your outcome, and not just intellectually—you need to *see it*, *feel it*, and *experience it* as if it's already yours. That level of clarity is what transforms a dream into reality.

Quite frankly, this is probably why many people feel stuck. If your Warrior has gotten tired, given up, or doesn't have a new vision, it's easy to fall into stagnation.

When you *know your outcome*—what you truly want—it gives your Warrior purpose and direction. It's the compass that keeps your Warrior focused, energized, and ready to tackle whatever comes your way.

Without that clarity, your Warrior can lose its way, like I did.

From the moment I entered the workforce, my Inner Warrior was in overdrive. It's the part of me that thrives on discipline, hard work, and relentless pursuit of a goal. It was my Warrior who pushed me to excel as a CPA, rise to partner in a firm with seventy-five employees, and manage the kind of responsibility that comes with helping clients navigate millions of dollars in tax liabilities.

My Warrior knew how to grind, how to achieve, and how to conquer the vision I'd set for myself.

But the same part of me that drove my success also pushed me toward destructive behaviors. I'd achieved so much, and I justified my actions as a "reward" for the work I'd put in. But my celebrations—binge drinking, partying until the early hours, and avoiding the consequences at home—were anything but empowering. My Warrior, unchecked and misaligned, was seeking certainty and escape in all the wrong places.

Looking back, I can see how my Inner Warrior was stuck in a loop of disempowering habits. Growing up, I'd been programmed to believe that drinking equaled fun. Alcohol was woven into every celebration, every stress-relief ritual, every moment of "letting go." As an adult, my Warrior clung to that programming, using alcohol to fill the gaps I wasn't ready to confront. My need for variety and release was being met in a way that only pushed me further from the life I wanted.

The breaking point came in October 2017, when my misaligned Warrior finally faced its reckoning. My decision to avoid coming home and instead crash at a buddy's house was my Warrior operating at its worst: avoiding the real battle that needed to be fought. My wife's ultimatum—quit drinking or I'm done—forced me to confront the reality that my Warrior had no clear vision. It was reacting, not leading.

In that moment, I realized my Warrior needed a mission, a purpose greater than just "getting through." My therapist helped me see that the first battle I needed to fight was for my family—and for myself.

The Warrior thrives on clarity, and I had to redefine my outcome. I didn't want my marriage to end, and I didn't want my kids to grow up seeing their dad check out when life got hard. So I made the promise to quit drinking and set a vision to repair what I had broken.

Jet Fuel: The Power of Vision

Since your Inner Warrior thrives on certainty, one of the most powerful ways to provide that certainty is through vision. Visualization is how you manifest the life you want—by seeing it, believing it, and taking intentional steps to make it happen.

If this sounds a little "woo-woo," stick with me. Chances are, you've already practiced this without even realizing it.

Think about a time you achieved a major success in your life. Maybe it was earning a degree, landing your dream job, or starting your own business. That success started with a vision—a clear outcome you wanted. Even if you didn't formally "visualize" it, the process was the same: you thought about what you wanted, pursued it, and made it a reality. That's manifestation in action, and it all begins with clarity.

When I bought my first condo, I didn't just see it as a home; I saw it as a stepping stone. It was in an up-and-coming area surrounded by new developments—schools, community centers, and, most exciting of all, multimillion-dollar homes being built right next door. Every day, I watched those homes rise from the ground, transforming from dirt lots into beautifully landscaped neighborhoods.

I'd see them and think, *One day, I'll live in a house like that.*

It was like having a real-life vision board, one I couldn't help but notice every day. That vision stuck with me. I didn't just wish for it; I set my sights on it. And a few years later, when all the construction was finished, Vika and I held the keys to one of those very homes.

My vision became a reality.

This is how your Inner Warrior operates. It craves certainty and works best when you give it a clear outcome. When you have a vision, you engage both your conscious and subconscious mind to align your actions and energy toward achieving it.

Whether you know it or not, you already have a vision—or multiple ones. Maybe you don't consciously know what they are, but if you're like me, you've always had a vision for something. That's why you've succeeded in certain aspects of your life. Perhaps that's why you run your own business, or have climbed the ladder of success is your field. It's certainly why you're a dad. You wanted something in life, you made a plan, and you conquered it.

I'm willing to bet you have your Inner Warrior dialed in. You went through school, earned a degree, landed a job, or maybe even started your own business. You followed the steps, tackled the challenges, and conquered the path that had been laid out before you.

But here's the real question: Was that path yours to begin with?

Not Your Vision

During a recent dentist visit, I asked my dentist why he chose his career. His answer?

"When I was eight years old, my dad started calling me Dr. David."

So, his dad had a vision for him to become a doctor—a vision he followed. But was it truly his? I didn't keep probing, but I should have asked him whether it was what he wanted.

This happens more often than we realize. Many of us follow a path laid out by someone else—our parents, society, or even our peers. Maybe you went to college because it was expected of you. Maybe you pursued a career because it was practical or because someone told you it was a good idea. But was it *your* idea? Was it your vision?

The life you've pursued may not even be your own.

The truth is, we're all programmed to some degree. Even under the best intentions, we are influenced (or expected) to reach certain goals or fulfill certain expectations.

For the majority of parents, they want what's best for their child. And the child, respecting and loving his or her parents, is deeply influenced by them. Despite the sweetest of intentions, we end up following a path that wasn't ours in the first place.

And if it's not our parents or other elders, we are influenced by our friends. You know the saying, *"You're the average of your five closest friends."* Whether we realize it or not, those around us impact our goals, our desires, our vision, and thus, our life. That then begs the question: Who do you surround yourself with, and how are they influencing you?

I'm not saying this to shame anyone. My point is to ask: *Are you living in alignment with your own vision, or someone else's?*

I wasn't spared from this programming either. Growing up, I was taught to get a good education, find a stable job, and avoid living paycheck to paycheck like my parents. These were noble goals, and they pushed me to achieve—but they weren't fully my own.

My siblings and most of my friends pursued a four-year college education because it was the thing to do—everyone did. The fact that society expects us to know what we want to do for a living at eighteen years of age is beyond me—but I digress.

Personally, I was drawn to business because it felt natural. My grandfather was an accountant, and though I never met him, I ended up following in his footsteps. (He worked for Arthur Anderson, the same firm where I eventually built my career.) I built a career in accounting, the "language of business," and achieved everything I was programmed to do.

But even after all that success, I didn't feel fulfilled.

Why? Because it wasn't truly *my* vision.

My vision was to become a successful business owner, and that vision came true. I didn't initially imagine owning an accounting firm, but I wasn't specific when I dreamed of success. I just wanted to be a "successful business owner," and I achieved that. But here's the thing—my vision wasn't complete. In my mind, being a successful business owner also meant being a happy and fulfilled husband and dad.

And that part? That part didn't come true.

What I had was success without fulfillment. So, when Tony Robbins said, "Success without fulfillment is the ultimate failure," at the first seminar I attended, it felt like he was speaking directly to me (more on this later).

My success as a business owner came with stress and overwhelm. By my late thirties, the more I achieved, the more I felt those pressures mount. Instead of joy and fulfillment, my achievements only brought more weight to carry. Something had to change.

If things had gone differently, society might have labeled this my midlife crisis. But for me, it wasn't a crisis—it was a wake-up call. It was time to redefine my vision, align it with what truly mattered, and finally make room for both success *and* fulfillment.

So, let me ask you: What's your vision? Maybe you don't have a clear answer yet, but you might know what you *don't* want—and that's a great place to start.

To simplify things, I break life into three primary areas. These are the foundations of your vision, and they're where your Inner Warrior can focus its energy for the greatest impact. Let's explore these next.

Your Primary Areas of Life

Establishing a vision is manifestation, but where do you start?

Many self-help gurus emphasize the importance of having a vision, but sometimes they make it unnecessarily complex. They insist we need a vision for every aspect of our lives, and some even expect us to conjure up twenty or more visions! Come on! Ain't nobody got time for that.

Allow me to simplify it for you with a Venn diagram of three circles.

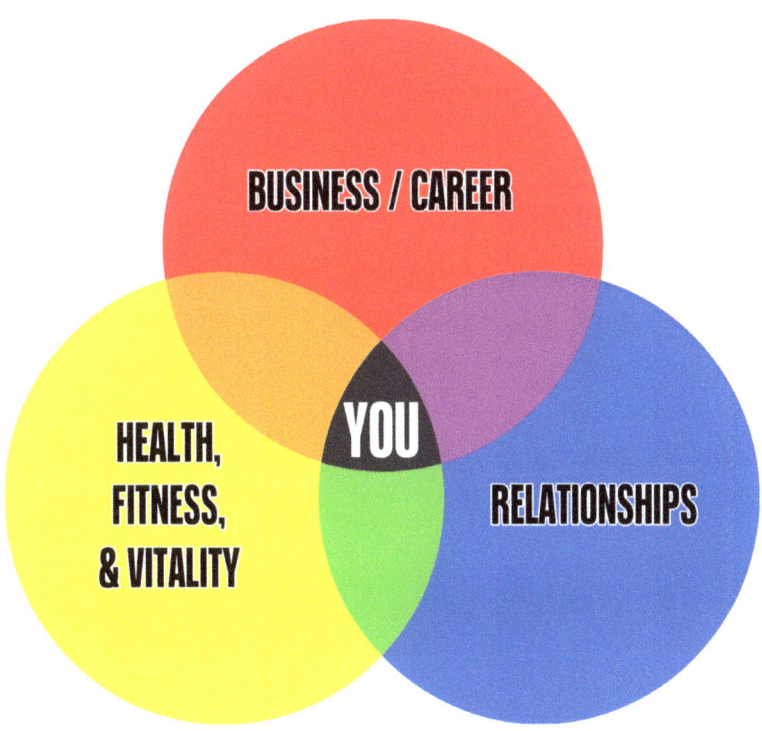

You, of course, are in the center of the three circles overlapping. The three circles represent the three primary areas of your life:

- Relationships
- Business/Career
- Health, Fitness, and Vitality

These are the foundational areas where you need clarity and vision. Let's briefly dive into each of these and why they are important.

Relationships

Humans are social creatures, and relationships are vital for both our happiness and our success. This circle represents all your relationships, starting with the one that likely came to mind first: your spouse or partner.

To be a great dad, you need a strong partnership. Navigating life is a team sport, and it's much easier (and more enjoyable) when you've got a solid teammate by your side. Take the time to define what a great relationship looks like for you. A strong relationship with your spouse or partner will make you not only a better husband but also a better father.

Beyond your spouse, there are other essential relationships:

- **Family**: Your parents, kids, and siblings are the core of your support system. These are often the first relationships we form, and they shape how we connect with the world.
- **Community**: Humans thrive in communities. Whether it's friends you've made through school, church, sports, or work, these connections enrich our lives. Friends provide support, laughter, and belonging.
- **Yourself**: Perhaps the most important relationship of all. The way you treat and value yourself directly impacts all your other relationships. A strong relationship with yourself lays the foundation for everything else in your life.

Business/Career

Your work—whether you're running your own business or working for someone else—should check two important boxes: it should meet your monetary needs *and* fulfill you.

Humans are wired to contribute. Accomplishment and productivity satisfy that Inner Warrior in us, giving us a sense of purpose and leaving the world better than we found it. Choosing the right career is critical because it supports the lifestyle you want and fuels your drive to do meaningful work.

For many, this is the area where they feel the most successful. That's because, from a young age, your Inner Warrior has likely been programmed to create and conquer a vision here. You've been taught to focus on your career, and chances are, you've done well. But it's worth asking yourself:

- Was this vision truly mine?
- Does my work still align with my purpose?

Maybe you've climbed the ladder but don't feel fulfilled. You're not alone. There's an epidemic of people working in jobs they don't love. But here's the good news: it's never too late to create a new vision. Unleash your Warrior, and start pursuing the work that truly speaks to your purpose.

And while we're talking about business and career, let's also talk about retirement. I question the whole idea of waiting until retirement to enjoy life. Why? Who decided that? Who came up with this plan where we're supposed to grind away for decades, save every penny, and then wait until we're older, exhausted, and maybe even physically limited to finally start living? It's like saying, "Let's postpone joy until we're too tired to fully embrace it."

For our generation, that old model—saving everything for retirement—feels outdated. Instead, we're realizing there's a better way. The focus now is on designing a life where work isn't just a means to an end. It's about asking, *How can I add value to the world while doing something fulfilling?* The goal is no longer trading time for money in a job you can't stand, but finding work that aligns with your passions, supports your lifestyle, and brings you joy—something you'd never want to retire from.

This is a total paradigm shift. We're not looking at retirement as the finish line anymore. Why would you retire if you genuinely enjoy what you're doing? The new question is: *How can I create a life that's sustainable, fulfilling, and full of purpose—forever?*

Health, Fitness, and Vitality

I love the saying, *"When you're healthy, you have a lot of goals. When you're not healthy, you only have one."* It's a reminder of how easy it is to take good health for granted until it's gone.

My goal is simple: never let it get to that point.

Your Inner Warrior is only as strong as the body carrying it. If you don't have the energy or capacity to pursue your vision, none of the other areas of life will thrive. That's why prioritizing your health is essential.

This means:

- Eating right
- Moving your body
- Getting enough rest

I know dads who have excelled in this area, making health a priority and setting an incredible example for their families. I also know dads who have completely neglected it. The truth is, as fathers, we are role models. Our actions speak louder than words, and when we prioritize our health, we teach our kids to do the same.

When you have clarity and vision in these three areas—relationships, career, and health—you create a solid foundation for your life. Each area is interconnected, and your Inner Warrior thrives when they are in harmony.

Three More Areas Emerge

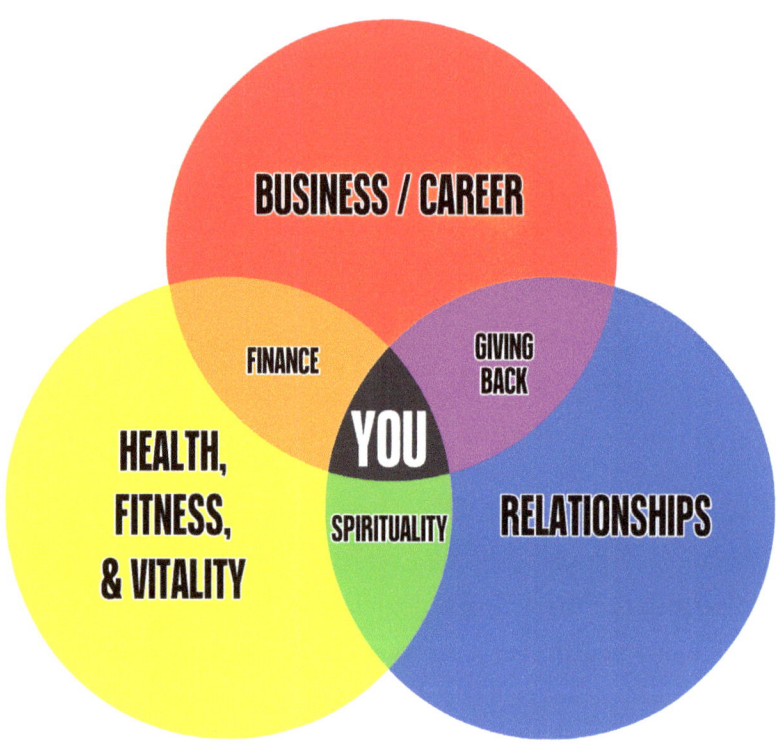

When you overlap the three primary areas—Relationships, Business/ Career, and Health, Fitness, and Vitality—three additional areas emerge at the intersections. These are distinct but equally important, as they connect the primary areas together. They are:

- Spirituality
- Giving Back
- Finance

Let's go over them.

Spirituality

Where the Relationships circle overlaps with Health, Fitness, and Vitality, we find Spirituality.

Doesn't that just make sense? A connection to the divine—whether you call it God, Spirit, or the universe—enriches your overall well-being. Spirituality ties into both relationships and vitality by giving your life deeper meaning and reminding you of your place in the grander scheme of things.

One of my favorite ways to reflect on spirituality is to think about the sheer vastness of the universe. Our galaxy, the Milky Way, has an estimated 100 billion stars—and researchers believe there are up to 200 billion *more* galaxies out there. Let that sink in. We're a speck, a blip in this unfathomable expanse, and yet, that realization can fill us with awe and gratitude.

Exploring spirituality can take many forms. It might involve a faith community like a church, mosque, temple, or synagogue. Or it could mean a deeply personal connection to God, a higher power, nature, or even art. Whatever it looks like for you, spirituality grounds you and gives your life purpose.

And like your sense of purpose, your spirituality will evolve. That's why it's important to revisit this area and adjust as needed—because staying connected to something bigger than yourself can transform your life.

Giving Back

Where Business/Career overlaps with Relationships, we find Giving Back.

This connection makes perfect sense. Your career enables you to earn money, and using that money to help others strengthens your relationships within the community—and even your relationship with yourself.

Humans are inherently altruistic. We're wired to help others, and giving back is one of the most powerful ways to connect, create positive change, and feel a deep sense of fulfillment. Whether it's donating money, volunteering your time, mentoring, or simply sharing an experience, giving back aligns your success with significance.

Take this example from my own life: In July 2023, I took my daughters, then twelve and fourteen, to a Taylor Swift concert in Los Angeles. It was unforgettable. The energy was electrifying, and my girls danced and sang their hearts out for three solid hours. Watching their faces light up with joy was like witnessing pure magic.

That night, I told my wife, "Every girl should experience this, and every parent should see that sheer joy on their child's face." She agreed but reminded me, "Not everyone gets that chance." She mentioned Sandra, our twelve-year-old neighbor, whose family was going through a tough time after her dad lost his job.

Without hesitation, I bought tickets for Sandra and her mom. Sharing that magic felt like the right thing to do—giving them an experience they might not have otherwise had. When I called Sandra's mom to let her know, she was overwhelmed with gratitude. "Are you serious?" she asked.

"Yes," I said. "Every parent should get to experience that magic with their child."

The day after the concert, she called to thank us. "You were right—it was pure magic. We'll never forget this. Thank you so much."

Giving back doesn't have to be complicated. It doesn't always mean donating large sums of money or volunteering for hours on end (though those are fantastic options). Sometimes, it's as simple as sharing an experience that brings joy to someone else's life.

Moments like these remind us that charity isn't just about giving—it's about connection, kindness, and creating memories that last a lifetime. After all, making someone else's world a little brighter is one of the most meaningful ways to align your success with something truly significant.

Finance

Finally, where Business/Career overlaps with Health, Fitness, and Vitality, we find Finance.

Your career directly impacts your financial health, and your financial health significantly affects your well-being. Stress about money—or the lack of it—can wreak havoc on your mental and physical health.

On the other hand, financial stability gives you the freedom to make choices that support a fulfilling and balanced life.

Financial health isn't about being rich; it's about being secure. It's about having a plan for unexpected expenses, reducing stress about money matters, and building the freedom to live on your terms. Ultimately, financial health gives you control over your future and the peace of mind that comes with it.

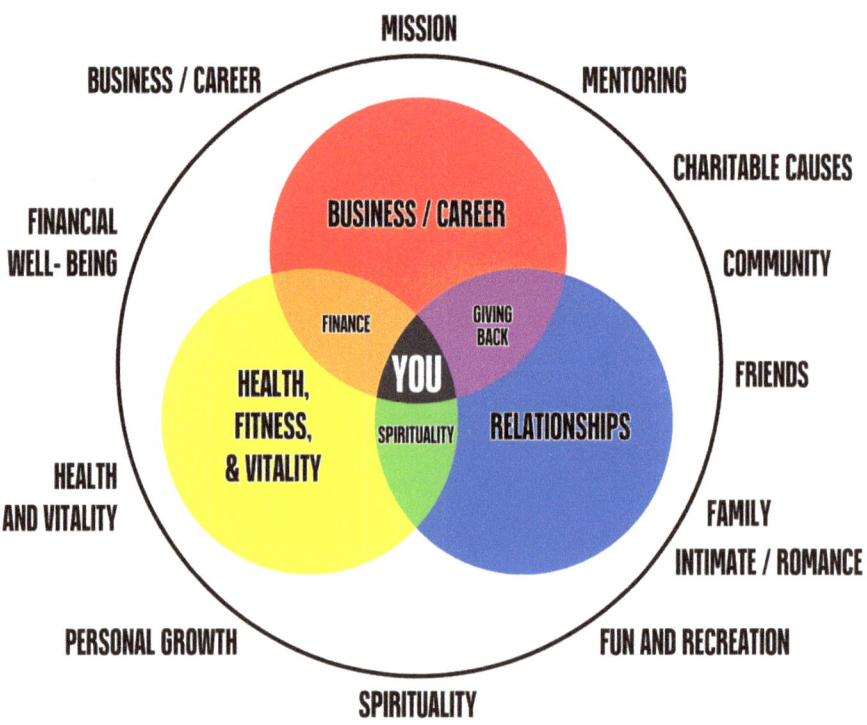

When you combine these three overlapping areas with the primary areas, you get six essential elements of life. Together, they encompass everything that truly matters. All those extra categories that some gurus emphasize? They all fall within these six areas.

So, now that we've simplified life into these core elements, what's next?

It's time to find the gaps.

Find the Gaps

Take a look at the Venn diagram and identify the areas where you feel there's room for improvement. Where are the gaps in your life? Creating a new vision is all about closing those gaps and moving toward greater alignment in one or more of the areas.

If it feels like there are huge gaps in every area, don't panic. You don't need to fix everything all at once—that's a recipe for overwhelm and burnout. Instead, pick one area to focus on. Start small, and spend as much time as you need making meaningful changes in that area. Slow, intentional progress is far more sustainable than trying to tackle everything at once.

For me, the biggest gap was in *relationships.* My relationship with my wife was suffering deeply, and I couldn't deny the cause: my drinking. It had caused her immense pain, and that wasn't the kind of relationship I wanted. I envisioned something completely different—a joyful relationship where we could laugh and cry together. A partnership built on unconditional love and trust, where we had each other's backs no matter what.

But that wasn't the reality. The truth was, our love had become conditional. I had broken her trust, and the pain I caused had driven our relationship to the brink. It wasn't what I wanted, but I had to own it: *this was my fault.*

Recognizing that gap was the first step. I could no longer ignore the damage I had caused or the fact that if I wanted to rebuild our relationship, I needed to take responsibility and make real changes.

This is what finding the gaps is all about—being honest with yourself about where you are now and where you want to be. Once you see the gaps clearly, you can start closing them, one step at a time. It's not about perfection. It's about progress and creating a life that aligns with your vision, your values (more on this in chapter 3), and the person you want to become.

So, where is your gap? Take the time to reflect. It's not about judgment or shame. It's about awareness and taking the first step toward transformation.

Setbacks: The Price of Growth

When some people quit an addiction, they quit cold turkey and never look back.

I was not one of those people.

When I promised my wife I would quit drinking, there was a little problem: I wasn't quitting for me—I was quitting for her. And we all know that's not how lasting change works. Predictably, I skirted my promise, only abstaining when she was around. This wasn't hard to pull off since I wasn't a daily drinker. I was an opportunistic binge drinker, seizing any chance to indulge when I thought I wouldn't get caught.

If I traveled overnight for work or if my wife was visiting family in Russia, out came the alcohol. And every time, I got hammered. I wasn't fully convinced I needed to stop drinking, and that deep-seated programming—associating alcohol with fun, relaxation, and escape—kept pulling me back.

In the eighteen months after my wife gave me the ultimatum, I binged four times.

Each time, I deeply regretted it.

One of the worst was during a work trip to Atlanta. I got blackout drunk with colleagues and employees—an experience cringeworthy enough on its own but exponentially worse when I had to face them the next day.

After each binge, I'd get angry at myself. That anger would fuel a renewed commitment to quit—until the next opportunity presented itself. My setbacks became a cycle of regret, self-loathing, and recommitment.

Here's the thing about being human: setbacks are part of growth. Disappointment, while painful, is a teacher. If we were perfect, life would be boring. That said, feeling disappointed in myself was far from fun. But I started to see each failure as a chance to grow and course-correct.

I knew my drinking was the primary reason for the gap in my marriage. I could see how it was sabotaging what I truly wanted: an unconditional, loving partnership.

Blacking out in Atlanta was not okay. Waking up with zero recollection of the night before in an unfamiliar city wasn't just embarrassing—it was dangerous. I had worked so hard to build my career, and one reckless decision could take it all away.

I wish I could say that was the last binge, but unfortunately, my recklessness didn't stop there. In early 2019, during my cousin's birthday celebration, I found myself desperately searching for a new way to have fun—anything to shake things up. My "brilliant" idea? Snorting cocaine.

Spoiler alert: cocaine did not fill the fun bucket.

The night started harmlessly enough. I had a beer, determined not to get blackout drunk like I had so many times before. Then someone offered me a bump. I thought, *Why not?* A few bumps later, I was buzzing—until I wasn't. At some point, I threw an edible into the mix, and by 4 a.m., the fun train derailed. By 7 a.m., with zero sleep, I was a wreck. I called my brother-in-law to drive me home and take my daughter to piano practice because I could barely function.

Later that day, when my wife, Vika, called to ask for a ride home from the airport, I told her to take an Uber—even though we live only five minutes away.

I couldn't face her. I couldn't face myself.

Vika had flown to Russia with her mom and brother for her dad's funeral, and she deserved to return to a husband who was present and steady—not the mess she came home to that day. That moment was a wake-up call. It was clear to me that she deserved better, my kids deserved better, and I deserved better.

That night, March 2, 2019, was the last time I drank.

The decision wasn't made lightly. I confided in my friend, Michael, sharing my fears about how I'd connect with my extended family during holidays when everyone else would be drinking. Michael, who accompanied me to a Tony Robbins event in Dallas later that year, encouraged me to try the Dickens Process—a powerful exercise designed to rewire your mindset and confront the real consequences of your choices.

It was some of the best advice I've ever received.

In those early days of sobriety, everything felt hard. Social situations were daunting. Alcohol was everywhere—at events, work functions, and family gatherings. I wondered how I'd relax, connect with others, or even have fun without a drink in hand.

That night marked the end of one chapter and the beginning of another—a journey toward becoming the version of myself I knew I could be. Sobriety was hard, but it was the turning point I desperately needed.

It set me on the path to real change.

A Done Deal: The Dickens Process

"Get comfortable!" Tony Robbins's thunderous voice boomed through the packed sports arena in Dallas. The energy was palpable—tense, electric, almost suffocating. The ten thousand of us, sardined into every seat and aisle, shifted nervously. We knew something big was coming, but none of us could have predicted the emotional roller coaster ahead.

"Lie down if you can—on the floor, in the aisles, wherever you need to. This is going to change your life."

It was July 2019, my first Tony Robbins event: *Unleash the Power Within.* I found a spot on the arena floor, wedged between rows of chairs. Others quickly followed, sprawling out in the narrow spaces as Tony's booming voice filled the space, commanding our attention. Up in the stands, participants settled into their seats, eyes closed, breathing deeply.

"Close your eyes," Tony ordered, his voice resonating like a drill sergeant who somehow made you feel safe despite the fear creeping into your gut. "We're going to do a visualization exercise called the Dickens Process."

The name comes from *A Christmas Carol* by Charles Dickens, where Scrooge is visited by the Ghosts of Christmas Past, Present, and Future. But this wasn't a cozy holiday tale. This was raw, brutal, and unapologetically intense.

"I want you to think about the ONE THING holding you back,"

Tony barked. "Maybe it's a limiting belief. Maybe it's a fear—fear of failure, fear of rejection, fear of love. Or maybe it's an unhealthy habit. WHAT is the ONE THING that is keeping you from becoming who you were meant to be? HOLD IT IN YOUR MIND!"

The room fell silent except for the shuffling of restless bodies. I closed my eyes and tried to focus. What was holding me back? My mind kept circling back to my drinking. It had been months since my last binge, but the shadow of it loomed over me. Was it really the thing?

Like anyone coming to terms with a bad habit, I justified it. From the outside, I was thriving—successful, a partner in my firm, living in a big house with a family I loved. Drinking hadn't *stopped* me, right? But then, a deeper truth rose up: my drinking was a wedge in my marriage. I craved a closer, more intimate relationship with my wife, Vika, but my drinking was sabotaging that vision.

"NOW," Tony shouted, his voice sharper, harsher, "I want you to think about what your life will look like ONE YEAR from now if you DON'T let go of this thing. Picture the WORST-CASE SCENARIO. WHAT IS THE WORST THING THAT COULD HAPPEN?"

A knot in my stomach appeared. My mind jumped to losing my job. Drinking had already gotten me in trouble before, and I knew how reckless I could be. Without my job, my family's entire lifestyle would unravel. We'd have to move to a smaller house, uproot my kids from their school and friends, downgrade our cars, cancel subscriptions—basically saying goodbye to everything we'd built.

My stomach churned with nausea as I imagined the ripple effect on my family. I could *feel* the loss in my body.

"NOW TAKE IT FURTHER!" Tony roared, his voice pushing deeper into my psyche. "What will your life look like FIVE YEARS from now if you KEEP doing this? WHAT PAIN WILL IT CAUSE? WHO WILL YOU LOSE?"

My gut-wrenching discomfort turned into a stomach punch. Five years of broken promises, of Vika's patience worn thin. I saw her leaving me. I saw myself alone, bitter, and disconnected from my kids.

The air in my lungs disappeared as panic gripped my chest. My mind raced through the aftermath—splitting custody, losing time with my daughters, watching them grow up without me as a constant presence.

And then Tony's voice came like a hammer: "WHO HAVE YOU LOST BECAUSE YOU REFUSED TO CHANGE?"

I pictured my kids turning away from me, their eyes filled with disappointment instead of love. It was a knife to the heart.

"NOW GO EVEN DEEPER!" Tony yelled, unrelenting. "TEN YEARS! What happens if you KEEP doing this? WHO SUFFERS? WHO DO YOU BECOME?"

The room erupted. The arena full of people screamed in anguish, sobbing uncontrollably. The collective energy of the arena was suffocating, the weight of ten thousand souls bearing their worst fears filling the space like a storm cloud ready to burst.

For me, the images darkened into a vivid, gut-wrenching vision. I saw my own funeral—not as a distant, abstract thought but as a painfully real scene playing out in my mind. My daughters stood there, side by side, their small frames shaking with sobs, their faces swollen and red from crying. Their grief was raw, consuming. They weren't just mourning the loss of their dad; they were mourning the life we could have shared.

I wasn't there to see their milestones. I wasn't there to walk them down the aisle on their wedding days, to cheer them on at their graduations, or to celebrate their triumphs. I wasn't there to offer advice when they faced challenges or to be the rock they could always count on. I was absent for the big moments, the small moments, *all* the moments.

My body shook uncontrollably. My chest heaved, my throat tightened, and tears swelled in the corners of my eyes. It was too much. The pain, the regret, the *finality* of those images consumed me.

This wasn't just about my life—it was about theirs. The choices I was making were robbing them of the father they deserved. I wasn't just gambling with my own future; I was stealing from theirs. That vision hit me harder than any physical pain ever could. It was unbearable, and I knew then and there that something had to change. My daughters needed more than the man I had become. They needed me alive, present, and whole. And for that to happen, I had to step up and let go of this thing that was holding me back.

NO WAY IN HELL, I thought. *NO WAY, NO HOW.*

Tony's voice softened but still carried the force of a freight train. "Now take a DEEP BREATH. Let go of these FALSE SCENARIOS."

The relief was instant, like a tidal wave washing over me.

"Those scenarios ARE NOT REAL," Tony continued, his tone firm but compassionate. "They WILL NOT happen—IF you let go of the thing holding you back. It's time to RELEASE IT. STEP INTO THE PERSON YOU NEED TO BECOME!"

I opened my eyes, trembling but resolute. The pain I'd felt was a wake-up call like no other. My drinking wasn't just a bad habit. It was a wrecking ball swinging toward everything I valued. I couldn't let it stay.

The Dickens Process sealed the deal. March 2, 2019, was the last time I drank, but this experience solidified my resolve.

When I stood up, the arena buzzed with the energy of ten thousand breakthroughs. The collective cries, screams, and awakenings reverberated in my chest. I walked out of that stadium that day not just relieved—but empowered.

No more drinking. No more holding back. Just pure, relentless forward motion.

Breaking Free: My Inner Warrior's Wake-Up Call

The Dickens Process was brutal—no sugarcoating it. It forced me to confront hypothetical scenarios so vivid, they felt painfully real. And that's the power of our minds: they can create physiological reactions in our bodies through thoughts alone. Those scenarios weren't real, but my body didn't know the difference. Thinking about my two daughters burying their dad because of something as senseless as alcohol hit me like a freight train.

That's what makes this exercise so powerful. It creates a nightmare scenario so vivid and so unbearable that it sparks real emotions. Emotions strong enough to drive action. My Inner Warrior needed that wake-up call—a no-holds-barred, gut-wrenching glimpse into what was at stake.

And it worked.

There was no way in hell I was ever going to touch alcohol again.

At first, I didn't want anyone to know I had quit drinking. I'd order sparkling water with lime so it looked like a vodka tonic. My therapist laughed at me when I told him. Looking back, it's almost comical, but it also shows how deeply I'd been programmed to believe alcohol equaled fun. Even more disturbing was the belief that if I didn't drink, I couldn't have fun.

How absurd is that?

The truth is, alcohol isn't the gateway to fun—it's a cheap, hollow substitute for real connection and joy. Breaking free of that belief was liberating.

The final nail in the coffin came from that Tony Robbins event, but none of it would have mattered if I didn't have a vision. My Inner Warrior needed something worth fighting for. That vision began with removing alcohol to improve my relationship with my wife, but the ripple effect changed everything: my relationship with my kids, my team at work, my clients, and my extended family all improved.

Now, more than six years later, my vision has evolved. My focus is on breaking the cycle of alcoholic programming for my children. I teach them that fun comes from love, connection, and giving—not from a bottle. We take trips, share experiences, and create memories that don't require alcohol to be meaningful.

I'm grateful to know they're growing up with a healthier view of what joy and connection truly look like.

And me? I no longer struggle at social events. In fact, I have more fun *not drinking* than I ever did with a drink in hand. No hangovers. No disrupted sleep. No hazy mornings filled with regret or stupidity.

Just clarity, connection, and confidence. Life is good!

Exercise: Create Your Vision

So, what's your vision?

It's time to dig deep and get brutally honest with yourself. Pull out the Venn diagram we've been working with and take a close look at each circle and overlapping area. Ask yourself:

- What do I want from my **health**?
- What do I want from my **relationships**?
- What do I want from my **career**?

Stop right here. Grab a pen and some paper, and take a moment to answer these questions. Writing your thoughts down isn't just an exercise; it's a powerful way to give your goals and desires shape and clarity. There's something transformative about seeing your words in front of you—it turns ideas into intentions and intentions into action. So don't just think about it; write it.

Then, consider the overlaps:

- How do I define **spirituality**?
- How can I give back through **charity**?
- What does **financial health** mean to me?

Again, stop to take a moment to write these down. Once you've assessed these areas, the next step is identifying your gaps. Where are you falling short? Which parts of your life feel the most disconnected from the vision you have for your future? Is it your health? Your relationships? Your career?

Once you've identified the area you want to work on, create a bold, unapologetic vision for what you want it to look like. Don't hold back. Dream big. Write down the ideal version of that part of your life. What do you want to achieve? How do you want to feel?

This exercise isn't about being realistic. It's about tapping into your deepest desires and creating a clear outcome that motivates and inspires you.

Now that you've got a sense of the gaps, let's turn to creating a vision for your future. And to do that, you'll recreate a version of the Dickens Process on your own.

Recreating the Dickens Process

1. **Identify what's holding you back.**

   Think about the one thing in your life that's preventing you from closing those gaps. Is it a bad habit, like overeating or drinking? Is it a limiting belief, like thinking you're not smart enough or capable enough? Or is it fear—fear of failure, rejection, or the unknown?

2. **Visualize the worst-case scenario.**

   Imagine your life if you don't let go of that thing. Start with one year from now. What's the absolute worst thing that could happen if you don't change? What does that look like? What does it *feel* like?

   Then, take it further: What would your life look like in five years? What would it look like in ten years?

3. **Don't hold back.**

   Feel the pain of staying stuck. Think about the impact it would have on your health, your relationships, your career, and your legacy. Feel it in your body—the heaviness in your chest, the knot in your stomach, the ache in your heart. Let it consume you for a moment.

4. **Turn the page.**

    Now, take a deep breath and let it go. Those scenarios are *not* your reality. They don't have to happen. But they're a powerful reminder of what's at stake if you don't change.

5. **Create your vision.**

    Close your eyes and imagine the opposite. Imagine your life in one, five, and ten years if you do close the gap. What does your health look like? Are you strong, energetic, and thriving? What do your relationships feel like? Are they deep, meaningful, and full of joy? What about your career—are you in a position that aligns with your purpose and provides financial stability?

    Paint the clearest picture possible. Imagine the details. Feel the pride, the love, the excitement, and the freedom of becoming the person you know you're meant to be.

Embracing Your Inner Warrior

Your Inner Warrior is a force to be reckoned with. It's the part of you that craves certainty and thrives on discipline, structure, and action. It's also the part of you that fights for the life you want—but only if you give it a clear vision to work toward.

The journey to empowering your Warrior isn't without its challenges. Setbacks will happen, and old habits or limiting beliefs will try to pull you back. That's part of the process. But every stumble is an opportunity to regroup, refocus, and push forward with even greater determination.

The key to activating your Inner Warrior is clarity. When you know your outcome—whether it's improving your health, strengthening your relationships, or building a more fulfilling career—you give your Warrior a mission. And when your Warrior has a mission, there's no limit to what you can achieve.

The Dickens Process wasn't the only life-changing experience I had during the four-day *Unleash the Power Within* event. In another session, I learned how to truly feel my feelings—something I'd never really done before. It was both terrifying and mind-blowing.

Fueled by inspiration, I eagerly joined Tony Robbins's annual membership. This gave me access to all of his programs, including a week-long event in Hawaii focused on improving relationships.

How perfect! I thought. *This is exactly what Vika and I need.*

I came home feeling like a new man. I couldn't wait to share everything I'd experienced with my wife—especially the conference I'd signed us up for. It was an opportunity for both of us to grow closer and for me to put my new skills to the test, particularly when it came to mastering my emotions.

That's where my journey was leading next. And as you'll see in the following chapter, mastering emotions is a key part of empowering your Inner Wizard and transforming your life.

CHAPTER 2

Your Inner Wizard: Mastering Your Emotions

"Conquer yourself rather than the world."
—*René Descartes*

WHEN I RETURNED FROM TONY ROBBINS'S *UNLEASH THE POWER WITHIN* in July 2019, I felt unstoppable. The event had left me electrified—intoxicated, even. Not on alcohol, but on life. I came home bursting with love, opportunity, and passion, like Ebenezer Scrooge waking up on Christmas morning.

Never again would I drink. I knew it in my bones, and I couldn't wait to share this revelation with my wife.

But while my Inner Warrior was charging ahead, putting the pieces in place to conquer my vision of repairing our relationship, Vika wasn't in the same place. In her eyes, I wasn't transformed—I was erratic, maybe even dangerous. And what unfolded next would test my ability to master my emotions like never before.

If you've never been to a Tony Robbins event, let me paint the picture. It's four days of intense energy, packed with seminars, breakthroughs, and life-changing inspiration. The man doesn't just *speak*—he *commands*. The energy from Tony and the crowd is so intoxicating that it's impossible to leave the same person you were when you arrived.

But it's also exhausting. Between the emotional roller coaster, the lack of sleep, and the constant movement, I came home physically depleted—but emotionally soaring. I was ready to save my marriage and take our relationship to the next level.

That's why, when I told Vika I'd signed us up for a week-long Tony Robbins relationship event in Hawaii, I expected her to be thrilled. Instead, her reaction was . . . less enthusiastic.

"What? Brian!" she snapped. "I don't want to go to that. Why are you drinking that Kool-Aid?"

Her skepticism didn't surprise me. Tony Robbins isn't for everyone, and I get it—he can come off as a bit of a showman. But in my eyes, if someone is inspiring people to grow and improve their lives, who cares if they're theatrical? I certainly didn't.

"Honey, you'll love it, I promise," I said, trying to soften her reaction. "We've talked about needing help. This is it. It'll be so good for us. You'll see."

But then she found out about the price tag: $85,000.

"Are you crazy? You didn't even consult me! I said we needed counseling, not some guru-type shit!"

Now, to be clear, the event itself didn't cost $85,000—that was for the annual membership to attend all of Tony's programs. But in my post-event euphoria, I'd jumped in with both feet. I believed this was the key to transforming not just our relationship, but my life as a whole.

And since my new vision was to improve my relationship, what better way than to attend an event together with my wife? I justified the price tag. Our relationship was worth it (and let's be honest, it was cheaper than divorce).

Unfortunately, no amount of explaining helped. We got into an argument and it escalated, fueled by my exhaustion from the intense Tony Robbins event. Dehydrated and sleep-deprived, I lost control.

Needless to say, I completely failed at mastering my emotions.

In her eyes, I seemed erratic. In reality, I was fine—just overwhelmed with excitement and perhaps a little delirious. Okay, maybe very delirious. Maybe even maniacal. Coupled with my lack of sleep and my utter excitement about my future without drinking, my wife thought I was hallucinating. Our argument grew in intensity, and my passion came off as erratic and frightening.

Vika thought I was high on drugs.

So, she did what anyone in their right mind would do: she called the cops.

So, there I was, stuck in a holding facility for three days, surrounded by people who *actually* were high. The blood test came back clean, of course, but policy was policy. It was humiliating, surreal, and the furthest thing from the triumphant homecoming I'd imagined.

If there's one thing I took away from that experience, it was this: *I needed to master my emotions.* My Inner Wizard—the archetype responsible for emotional intelligence and self-regulation—was nowhere to be found when I needed it most.

Eventually, Vika agreed to attend the Hawaii event. I made a deal with her. "If you hate it," I told her, "I'll take you on a European vacation to make it up to you." She reluctantly agreed, and I silently hoped that this experience would be the thing to pull us back from the edge. I'm sure the location helped her decision, but it didn't mean she trusted me yet. Our relationship was still on thin ice, and those three months between the events were some of the hardest of my life.

Vika was stuck in the past, replaying old stories of my drinking and the pain I'd caused her. And to be fair, I'd given her plenty of ammunition over the years. Her loops of distrust and disappointment were ingrained, and no amount of talking could change that.

While I came home as Ebeneezer, Vika still saw me as the binge drinker.

I tried explaining my transformation, my commitment, my vision for our future. But in her eyes, I was just another guy drinking the Tony Robbins Kool-Aid.

If the Inner Warrior thrives on action and discipline, the Inner Wizard thrives on wisdom, clarity, and emotional mastery. It's the part of you that knows how to navigate difficult conversations, remain calm under pressure, and lead with empathy instead of ego.

In those three months, I realized I had a lot of work to do—not just in proving my transformation to Vika, but in proving it to myself. I needed to stop reacting and start listening. I needed to learn how to process my feelings without letting them boil over. I needed to build the kind of trust and connection that could only come from true emotional mastery.

But what became painfully clear in those months was this: *I wasn't the only one who needed to master my emotions.*

The Breakthrough Moment

The relationship event took place in Hawaii, surrounded by breath-taking landscapes and the warmth of tropical breezes—a stark contrast to the heavy emotional baggage so many of us carried into those sessions. Hundreds of couples attended, all seeking the same thing: to enhance, improve, or save their connection with their partner.

Vika and I were no different.

In one session, Tony called a couple to the stage—a pair who seemed to be even closer to the brink than we were. The husband looked desperate for change, while the wife radiated a deep reluctance, as if she didn't even want to be there.

Tony began by addressing the husband. "This is a safe space," he said. "Unleash your frustrations. I'm here to help."

The floodgates opened. Years of bottled-up anger, hurt, and disappointment poured out of him. He admitted how his frustrations with his wife had led him to treat her poorly, perpetuating a toxic cycle.

Then Tony turned to the wife. "And you?" he asked gently but firmly. "How are *you* contributing to this dynamic?"

She stiffened, unable to meet his gaze. Slowly, the truth emerged: she kept a meticulous notebook documenting every mistake her husband had ever made. Every argument. Every perceived slight.

Apparently, her therapist had advised her to keep this grim record of grievances.

"Do you think this notebook is serving you?" Tony asked, his voice steady and loving but unrelenting. "Is it helping your relationship? Or is it holding you back?"

The room held its collective breath.

Tony has this way of speaking—real, raw, but not cruel. He doesn't sugarcoat, but he also doesn't tear people down.

The wife hesitated, and then, something shifted. She admitted that clinging to these past wrongs was keeping them trapped in a loop of pain. By keeping score, she was stifling any hope of progress.

That's when Tony introduced a Hawaiian tradition called *ho'oponopono*. He guided the couple through its four transformative phrases: "I love you. Please forgive me. I'm sorry. Thank you."

They repeated the words, their voices trembling, their walls breaking down. In front of hundreds of strangers, they chose to let go of their wounds and start anew.

Their story hit me like a lightning bolt. The wife's grudges mirrored Vika's. I saw how my drinking, my lies, and my selfishness had scarred her. But I also realized how holding onto those stories was keeping her stuck.

I turned to Vika. For the first time in what felt like forever, I didn't see the distance between us. Instead, I saw her—the woman I loved, the partner I wanted to fight for. With my heart pounding in my chest, I took her hands in mine. Her eyes met mine, and I summoned every ounce of love and sincerity I could muster.

"I love you," I began, but my eyes and presence carried the weight of what I truly meant: *I love you more than words could ever express.*

I then said, "I am sorry." But in my heart, I was apologizing for so much more—for the nights she stayed up worrying about me, for the promises I broke, for putting my selfish habits above our family. I was silently saying, *I'm sorry for acting like a man-child, for making you feel like you had to carry the weight of this relationship alone.*

Next, I said, "Please forgive me." Though I didn't articulate it in that moment, my soul was asking for forgiveness for every time I failed to put her first, for every moment I broke her trust.

Finally, I said, "Thank you." But the gratitude ran deeper than the words. My soul was thanking hers for standing by me, for believing in the man I could become even when I fell short.

I repeated those same four phrases ten times. And then she repeated the phrases to me ten times.

It was the most powerful exercise I have ever experienced—raw, humbling, and transformative. A moment of pure connection where our words and presence healed what had been fractured.

In that moment, something shifted. I could feel it. The weight of my past actions didn't disappear—it wasn't magic—but the tight grip it had on Vika's heart began to loosen. The hurt we had carried for so long started to evaporate, replaced by something warm and hopeful.

We embraced, and the world around us faded. It felt like we'd silently renewed our vows right there in the seminar.

Letting Go of the Past

We all hold onto stories—narratives that keep us trapped in emotional states that feel familiar, even if they don't serve us. Vika had been replaying the story of my drinking, of my broken promises, of the pain I caused her. But for the first time, she recognized it.

She let go.

Instead of being controlled by those emotions, she allowed herself to embrace new ones. Even if those emotions felt uncomfortable, they were the key to leaving the past behind.

By the end of the event, Vika saw the value. She loved the seminar— and I swear it saved our marriage.

As we boarded the plane back home, we left more than just Hawaii behind. We left behind the hurt, the resentment, and the baggage that had been weighing us down for years. In their place, we carried something far more precious: a shared vision for the future and the renewed warmth of a love that had weathered the storm.

That deal I made with Vika? No European vacation was needed. Hawaii had been more than enough.

The lessons from *ho'oponopono* and that week transformed not just our relationship, but how we approached life. Vika and I were finally ready to move forward—together.

Meet Your Inner Wizard

Cultivating your Inner Wizard is about mastering the magical ability to use your emotions to serve you. When you unlock this power, you'll find that everything in life sucks less. You'll navigate challenges with love, ease, and clarity—and create deeper connections with the people around you.

But let's be real: mastering your emotions is easier said than done. It takes work. It requires self-awareness, intentionality, and the willingness to break free from old patterns.

You see, your emotions are powerful, but they're also tricky. Left unchecked, they'll run the show, steering you into reactive loops that don't serve you. Think about those Snickers commercials—you're not you when you're hangry, right? Instead of solving the real issue, advertisers want you to mask it with a candy bar. The same goes for stress eating, doom-scrolling on your phone, or snapping at someone when you're overwhelmed. These are all emotional responses that feel good in the moment but keep you stuck in patterns that don't align with your best self.

Fueling Your Inner Wizard

Your Inner Wizard needs the right ingredients to work its magic. What you put into your body and mind matters. Nourish yourself with good nutrition, consume uplifting or constructive media, get regular exercise, and prioritize sleep. Every doctor on the planet will tell you to do these things for your health, but I'm telling you to do them for your Wizard.

When your Inner Wizard has the right tools, it can create the formula to help you conquer depression, anger, stress, and overwhelm. With a strong foundation, your Wizard can guide you through life's chaos with a steady hand and a loving heart.

My wife was stuck in a loop. She kept reliving the nightmares I had put her through—over and over. The emotions of doubt, distrust, anger, and skepticism were like a familiar playlist on repeat.

Even though those emotions weren't pleasant, they were *familiar*. And familiarity feels safe. Our subconscious clings to what it knows, even when it's unhealthy. For Vika, those emotions became her default setting, a way of calming her mind and body by sticking to the known rather than venturing into the uncertain.

Here's the thing: our subconscious minds are wired for safety, and safety often feels like staying put. Change—no matter how positive—feels risky because it's unfamiliar. This is why so many of us get stuck in patterns that don't serve us.

Even though I had apologized and committed to going sober (for real this time), Vika struggled to envision a new future for us because she was still replaying the past.

In October 2019, something shifted. Vika recognized her pattern and decided to let it go. She saw that holding onto those emotions wasn't serving her or our relationship. It was a moment of profound release, the kind of transformation that comes when you stop letting your emotions control you and start rewriting your story.

The Stories We Tell Ourselves

What story are you telling yourself? How does your mind and body react to that story?

Let's be clear: I'm not saying you should suppress your emotions. Quite the opposite. You need to feel your emotions, to sit with them and understand them. Suppression doesn't work—it backfires. What I mean by mastering your emotions is this: being so rooted in who you are that when life throws chaos your way, you can respond in a way that aligns with your vision (Inner Warrior) and values (Inner King, coming in chapter 3).

Sometimes mastering your emotions means biting your tongue in the heat of an argument. Other times, it's about finding the courage to speak up and communicate your needs clearly. It's not about ignoring how you feel; it's about being intentional with your reactions.

Mastering your emotions means finding a state of equilibrium. It's about stepping back from reactivity and taking a moment to examine the situation in 3D. What's really happening here? What's the underlying truth? How can you respond in a way that serves you, instead of getting swept away by the mess of raw emotion?

Your Inner Wizard thrives on this kind of wisdom and clarity. When you activate it, you become the person who pauses before reacting, who sees the bigger picture, and who chooses actions aligned with their vision.

That brings us to a deeper question: Where do emotions come from, anyway?

Let's explore.

Jet Fuel: The Triangle of Beliefs

So, where do emotions come from? The answer might vary depending on how deep you want to dive, but for the purposes of this book, they stem from one key source: your beliefs.

And what is a belief? A belief is nothing more than a feeling of certainty about how things *ought* to be.

And this is where we get ourselves into trouble.

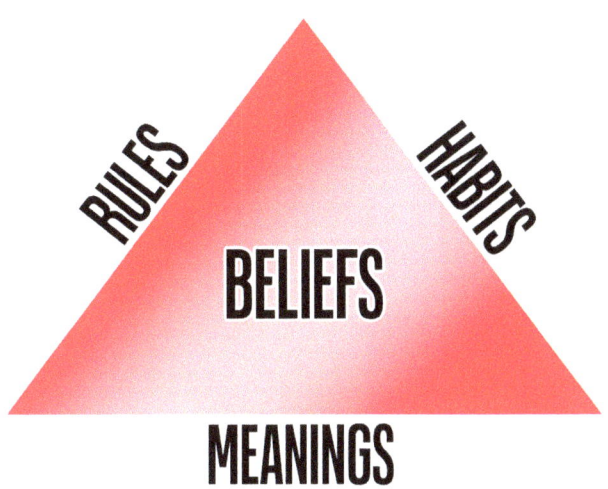

Our belief system isn't something we create in a vacuum. It comes from a variety of people, places, and experiences. Growing up, we're programmed with certain beliefs by our families, teachers, and the culture around us. As we get older, those beliefs often evolve—or in some cases, change completely.

But no matter where your beliefs come from, they all root themselves in three key areas: *meanings, rules,* and *habits.* Together, they form what I call the Triangle of Beliefs—a framework that governs how we experience the world and, in turn, how we respond emotionally.

Let's break down each piece of the triangle.

Meanings: The Drivers of Emotion

One evening over dinner, a friend shared that his sister had filed for divorce.

"Oh, I'm happy for her," I replied casually.

My response didn't sit well with him. His face tightened, and I could tell he was holding back some choice words. I didn't mean to be disrespectful, but it quickly became clear that we had assigned completely different meanings to the same event.

To him, divorce meant pain and loss. It symbolized the heartbreak of a failed marriage, and he felt deep sympathy for his sister. To me, divorce often signals relief and a fresh start. If things weren't working out between the couple, then separation could be the best path forward.

Same event, completely different meaning.

We attach meaning to everything in life, and those meanings shape our emotions. Take death, for instance. If a stranger dies, the emotional impact is likely brief and detached—an acknowledgment of loss, perhaps a moment of empathy, and then you move on. But if a close family member dies, the meaning shifts entirely. The loss becomes profound, personal, and deeply felt.

The event itself doesn't change. What changes is the meaning we assign to it.

And that's the crux of it: *you are in control of the meaning you assign.* The meaning you choose leads directly to how you react and feel. Once you realize you're the author of your emotions, you can take ownership of them—and better manage them.

Let's bring it closer to home. Imagine someone cuts you off on the freeway. What's your immediate reaction? If you're like most people, it's something like, "What a jerk!" or "Hey, buddy, learn how to drive!"

But let's pause for a moment. Is it true that this person is a jerk? Do you have all the evidence to conclude they're a terrible driver?

No, you don't.

Before I learned to master my emotions, I was a classic case of road rage. When someone cut me off, I'd turn into Brian the Defender—a self-appointed hero of freeway justice. My mission? Letting the offender know their actions were unacceptable. This often included flipping the bird, shouting obscenities, and maybe tailgating for good measure.

Then one day, I flipped the scenario.

What if *I* was the one who cut someone off? I'm not a reckless driver, but mistakes happen. Maybe I didn't see them in my blind spot, or maybe I was rushing to the hospital because a loved one was in critical condition.

In either case, I wouldn't label myself a jerk or a bad driver.

That realization hit me hard. I was forty-two years old before I finally learned that when someone cuts me off, *they don't get to decide how I respond. I do.*

We own our emotions. What a revelation!

When you're learning to master your own emotions, think of yourself as the Merriam-Webster dictionary. Just like the dictionary defines words, you define the meaning you assign to events. Those definitions, in turn, create the emotions you feel.

The great news? You can always redefine the meaning.

Start by examining the meanings you've assigned to situations. What story are you telling yourself? Why do you believe it? What emotions are those meanings producing?

You can't fix something without understanding what it means to you first. But once you figure it out, you can rewrite the meaning—and rewrite your emotional response.

Here's the big takeaway: *you own your emotions.* Your reaction is *your choice.* The power lies with you, not the person who cuts you off, not the friend who disagrees with you, and not the boss who overlooks your hard work.

The meanings you assign to events shape your reality. Choose them carefully, because they'll determine whether you experience anger or peace, despair or hope, stagnation or growth.

Mastering your Inner Wizard means being intentional with the meanings you create. When you own this process, you don't just react to life—you actively shape it.

Rules: The Framework for Your Emotions

Whether you realize it or not, your emotions are governed by rules you've created. These rules dictate when and how you allow yourself to feel happiness, love, success, or acceptance. Often, these rules are a product of our upbringing, subconscious programming, or external influences.

But here's the rub: many of these rules are tied to things completely outside of our control.

I'll give you an example: the stock market.

I've got money in the stock market, and there was a time when those numbers on a screen had total control over my emotions. If the market was up, I was on top of the world. If it was down, I was anxious, stressed, and second-guessing everything. Should I sell? Should I buy more? It's almost laughable how consumed I was by it.

It hit me one day: *how cheaply I let my emotions be swayed.*

The stock market doesn't care about Brian Gray. It doesn't know my hopes, dreams, or goals. It's going to rise and fall regardless of what I do, and no amount of worrying or obsessing will change that.

When I realized I'd created a rule that tied my emotional state to something I had zero control over, I knew I needed to change it. So, I let go of all the rules I had tied to things beyond my influence.

Take a moment and think about the rules you've created for yourself. What are your rules for happiness? For success? For love? Are they tied to things you can control, or are they dependent on external factors?

Here are some of the old rules I used to live by:

- I will be happy when I have financial abundance.

Growing up in a household that lived paycheck to paycheck, I developed a belief that money was the key to happiness. But when I achieved financial abundance, happiness didn't magically appear. It was a hollow victory.

- I will be accepted if people tell me they like me.

In my quest for acceptance, I sought validation through money. During the late nineties' .com boom, I made a lot of cash. To earn people's approval, I'd pick up tabs at dinners, loan money to friends, and act as though generosity could buy connection. It didn't.

- I will be successful when I make it to partner.

When I became a partner in my firm in 2014, I expected to feel successful. Instead, it felt like the goalposts had moved again. I told myself, *You'll feel successful when you become an equity partner.* Six years later, when I finally achieved that milestone, the feeling was still absent. Success isn't a destination, and I had been chasing an illusion.

- I will feel loved when my wife showers me with gifts and affection for no reason.

This one's my favorite because of how ridiculous it sounds now. I had this Hollywood-inspired idea that love should come in grand gestures and endless affection. When Vika didn't meet my unrealistic expectations, I got moody and resentful.

After learning to master my emotions, I rewrote my rules. I realized the old ones were giving all the power to external factors—things I couldn't control. I shifted my focus inward, creating rules that aligned with what I could influence: my own actions and attitudes.

- I will be happy anytime I smile at someone.
- I will be accepted anytime I take action to let people be heard.
- I will be successful anytime I wake up and do a morning exercise.
- I will feel love anytime I am grateful for all the blessings in my life.

These new rules brought a sense of freedom. Now, I don't rely on others to dictate how I feel. I feel love when I *give* love. I feel accepted when I *accept* others. I feel happy when I *make others happy*. I feel successful when I *see others succeed*.

The shift from external to internal control has been life-changing. The old rules were rigid, dependent on things I couldn't command. The new ones are fluid, empowering, and entirely within my grasp.

Take a moment to reflect on your own rules. What have you told yourself about happiness, love, success, or acceptance? Are these rules serving you, or are they holding you back?

Remember: your rules are yours to create. If they aren't working for you, rewrite them.

Habits

When my Inner Warrior was running the show, coming home was a predictable script—and not a good one.

As soon as I walked through the door, my wife or kids would ask, "How was your day?"

Without skipping a beat, I'd answer, "Exhausting." Or maybe, "Awful. My partner pissed me off."

Whatever the story, it was a downer.

Who was I inspiring with those answers? No one! No wonder my wife didn't want to engage with me in the evenings. My replies were conversation killers.

But in my mind, I had it all twisted. I thought that by sharing how terrible my day was, I was signaling, *Brian needs love and comfort.* Naturally, I expected my wife to respond with instant affection. But when that didn't happen, my Inner Warrior's quick fix was to grab a beer.

The first sip was like a magic eraser for stress. The pressures of the day dissolved, leaving me in a mellow, melancholy state—a feeling I bizarrely enjoyed. Feeling like I was now "on her level," I'd go over to hug my wife.

But I wasn't on her level. She wasn't sipping away her stress, and my manufactured calm didn't resonate with her. When she didn't return the energy, I'd sulk, jump to conclusions—*She doesn't understand me!*—and then grab another beer.

It was a vicious loop.

Here I was, the achiever, working hard every day to create a great life for my wife and kids. Yet my habits—the way I managed my emotions—were driving them away.

Your emotions are habitual.

It's true. Emotions are habits. We get stuck in emotional loops, reacting the same way to similar triggers, over and over again. It's not conscious—it's automatic. But once I realized my emotional habits, I had a choice: keep replaying that loop, or rewrite the script.

Even if work was exhausting, I didn't need to bring that energy home. I could choose a different energy. So, I did.

And let's be real: we're all exhausted. Life is exhausting. But that's not a bad thing. It means you're living. Now, when I pull into the driveway, I take a moment. I remind myself of the family waiting for me inside—the people I love most in this world. So, instead of saying, "The day beat me up," I now say, "I gave this day my all." When my wife or kids ask about my day, I don't unload my stress on them. Instead, I say something like, "It was a great day, but I'm even more excited to hear about *your* day!"

At the end of an exhausting day, I look at my wife and say, "That was a day well-lived."

Take a moment to reflect:

- What emotions do you feel most often?
- What triggers those emotions?
- Are those emotions serving you—or are they keeping you stuck?

We all have emotional loops. Some keep us inspired, while others drag us down or alienate the people around us. If you're like most people, your "favorite" emotions might not even align with the ones you experience daily.

When I ask people what their favorite emotion is, they always name a positive one—joy, love, gratitude. But if I ask whether that's their reality, the answer is usually no. They're stuck in stress, frustration, or sadness instead.

Here's the good news: you can choose your emotions. You can change your emotional habits by changing the scripts you're playing.

Instead of letting your emotions run on autopilot, take control. Start by identifying the triggers that set off those old loops. Then decide how you want to respond instead. When you do, you'll notice a ripple effect. The energy you bring into a room will inspire the people around you. Your family, your friends, your team—they'll all feed off the positive energy you're creating.

Your Inner Wizard thrives on this power: the ability to choose your emotional state and inspire others to do the same.

Exercise: Your Habitual Emotions

Grab a piece of paper and fold it in half. Take a moment to reflect on the emotions you've experienced over the past week. On the right side, list the positive emotions you've felt—like happiness, joy, peace, or love. On the left side, list the disempowering ones—such as anger, overwhelm, anxiety, sadness, or frustration.

Now, don't just skim past this exercise—really take the time to do it. Grab your phone, set a timer for two minutes, and write down all the positive emotions you've felt in the past week. Maybe you felt peaceful because you finally had a quiet moment to read this book. Perhaps you felt excited to learn something new. Most people find it challenging to think of more than ten empowering emotions, but give it your best shot.

Once you've completed your list of positive emotions, reset the timer for another two minutes. This time, write down all the negative emotions you've experienced over the past week. Maybe you felt stressed because your to-do list keeps growing. Perhaps you felt anger toward a boss or client who seemed unreasonable. Or maybe you felt overwhelmed by the state of the world, your finances, or just life in general.

Once you've finished, circle one emotion from each list:

- The *positive emotion* you felt the most this week.
- The *disempowering emotion* you felt the most this week.

You should now have two emotions—one from each side. Out of those two, which one dominated your week? Which one did you feel more often?

Congratulations, you've just identified your *favorite emotion.*

And here's the surprising part: for most of us, it's the one from the negative list.

My favorite emotions were overwhelm and frustration. When I came home saying, "I'm exhausted," that was overwhelm talking. When I complained about my partner, that was frustration rearing its head. Those emotions were so ingrained, they felt automatic—a default setting I didn't even realize I had.

The quality of your life is determined by the quality of your habitual emotions.

So, take a hard look at your lists. What emotions aren't serving you? What emotional habits have you created? Some of these habits you may have adopted unconsciously—from your parents, your school, your church, or even society's expectations.

These loops are deeply embedded, but the good news is, they're not permanent. You can identify them, rewrite them, and create new, empowering habits.

This process isn't quick, and it's not one-and-done. Rewriting your emotional habits takes time, practice, and patience. It's a continual process of self-awareness and growth. Even now, I'm still identifying old habits and creating new ones.

The habits you build aren't just for you, either. You're building them for your kids, too.

I don't want my kids to inherit my old, unproductive emotional loops. I don't want them to equate love with gifts or affection with appeasement. I want them to navigate the world with emotional resilience, self-awareness, and clarity—tools I've worked hard to cultivate in myself.

Every time you rewrite an emotional loop, you're not just improving your own life. You're teaching the people around you—especially your children—that it's possible to break free from old patterns. You're modeling what it means to choose empowerment over frustration, joy over overwhelm, and love over fear.

What will your emotional legacy be? Take the time to figure it out, one habit at a time.

The Gratitude Hack

One of the fastest ways to master your emotions is to harness the power of gratitude. Gratitude is a game-changer. It can shift your emotional state in an instant, pulling you out of frustration, overwhelm, or despair.

As author Dr. Joe Dispenza says: *Where focus goes, energy flows.*

The secret to escaping the grip of low emotions? Find something—anything—to be grateful for. The moment you feel anger, overwhelm, or anxiety creeping in, pause. Take a deep breath and ask yourself: *What can I be grateful for right now?*

I promise you, it works.

Let's return to me and my road rage, for example. Before mastering my emotions, I was a serial road rager, losing it every time someone cut me off. Now, instead of letting anger take the wheel, I go straight to gratitude:

> *I'm grateful that guy didn't hit my car.*

> *I'm grateful that traffic is slow so that I had enough time to brake.*

That simple shift rewires the entire experience. What could've been a stressful, anger-fueled spiral turns into a moment of calm and clarity.

Gratitude is the greatest hack in the world. Whenever you're feeling disempowered, just stop and think of something you're thankful for. It can be anything, big or small.

> *I'm grateful for the sun that is shining today.*

> *I'm grateful for the connection I made with my kids this morning at breakfast.*

> *I'm grateful I have a roof over my head.*

> *I'm grateful for toilet paper.*

Seriously, toilet paper. Try living without it and see how much you miss it!

Gratitude doesn't have to be complicated—it just has to be intentional. When you're in a state of gratitude, it's physiologically impossible to feel stress at the same time. Gratitude changes your brain chemistry, pulling you out of fight-or-flight mode and into a place of serenity.

Disempowering emotions like stress, overwhelm, judgment, and comparison are all *inside jobs.* They're emotions we create and feed, often without realizing it. But gratitude is the ultimate antidote.

Mastering My Emotions

Keeping my promise to Vika about not drinking wasn't what saved our marriage. *Mastering my emotions* did. I was in control of my emotions. I could decide how I wanted to feel.

It only took me forty-two years to figure this out! Why didn't anyone teach us this in high school?

As I practiced this newfound skill, my confidence grew across every area of my life. I began to apply my Inner Wizard to every situation.

Take my clients, for example. In the past, I dreaded dealing with unhappy ones. If they were stressed or upset, it made me anxious, and I'd avoid them like the plague. By not addressing their concerns proactively, I made things worse.

Now, I take a completely different approach. When a client is unhappy, I address it head-on. I tell them, "I want you to be happy. Let's solve this problem together. If, in the end, you're still not satisfied, you don't have to pay our full rate—but we won't continue working together either."

Funny thing happened when I implemented this: I no longer have unhappy clients.

By mastering my emotions, I became better at guiding clients through their own. When they'd spiral into emotional decision-making, I'd stay calm and pragmatic, helping them focus on what was best for their family or business.

This skill is critical for all of us, not just in business, but in life. Chris Voss, a former hostage negotiator, highlights this in his book *Never Split the Difference*. He says, *"If you can't control your own emotions, how can you expect to influence someone else's?"*

That insight struck a chord. Whether you're negotiating a business deal or navigating your child's meltdown, emotional mastery is the foundation for influence and connection.

And as fathers, it's our responsibility to pass this skill on to our children.

The Key to Fulfillment

Tony Robbins delivered a truth bomb at that first event: *"If you have success without fulfillment, that is the ultimate failure."*

That hit me like a 2x4.

I had success—a big house, a thriving business, a beautiful family—but I wasn't fulfilled. I was living proof of what Tony described: the ultimate failure. Thankfully, my Inner Wizard showed me another way. The key to fulfillment wasn't external—it was internal. It was mastering my emotions.

Mastering my emotions taught me that I could feel whatever I wanted, whenever I wanted. If I want to feel happy, I simply recall a memory that makes me happy—and boom! Happiness washes over me. If I want to laugh, I know where to find that, too. And when life gets tough, I go straight to gratitude.

You can do this, too.

Mastering your emotions doesn't mean ignoring or suppressing them. It means understanding where they come from and taking control. Most of our emotions stem from the gap between how we think things *ought* to be and how they actually are.

But *who says the way you think things ought to be is right?* Just because I believe something should go a certain way doesn't mean the universe agrees. And I'm okay with that.

Mastering emotions isn't a one-and-done deal. It's a process—a muscle you strengthen with time and effort. I haven't uncovered all my unproductive habits yet, and that's fine. We're dynamic people living in dynamic, ever-changing environments. That means continually reassessing our habits, identifying which ones aren't serving us, and replacing them with better ones.

It takes practice. You won't conquer it all in one day. But the work is worth it. This journey isn't over—it never will be. But every step forward brings more alignment, more fulfillment, and more joy.

Mastering my Inner Wizard gave me access to my true King. It wasn't until I developed the emotional control of a wizard that I could fully step into the clarity and decisiveness of a king. And from this empowered place, I was finally able to define my values—the foundation for everything we'll explore next.

CHAPTER 3:

Your Inner King: Know Your Values

"Your core values are the deeply held beliefs that authentically describe your soul."
—John C. Maxwell

"It's not hard to make decisions when you know what your values are."
—Roy E. Disney

"HEY, BRIAN—HAVE YOU HEARD ABOUT THE SCHOOLS PUTTING litter boxes in their bathrooms for students who identify as cats?"

This question came out of nowhere during a client meeting. We'd been reviewing taxes when he dropped this bombshell.

"What? Are you serious?" I nearly fell off my chair.

"It's true," he insisted. "I saw it on the news. Apparently, they call these kids 'furries.'"

I stared blankly at him as a surge of judgment and anger welled up inside me. My blood boiled. *Furries? Litter boxes in schools? What has this world come to?*

When the meeting ended, I left his office feeling disturbed and unsettled. My emotions were all over the place—confusion, anger, disbelief. But instead of spiraling, I took a deep breath and gave myself a moment to practice what I preach: mastering my emotions.

Why was I so triggered?

I decided to dig deeper. Who was the villain in this story?

Was it the school? No. Schools have to navigate complex societal issues every day, doing their best with what they have.

Was it the kids? Also no. Children love to pretend, push boundaries, and explore their imaginations. That's part of being a kid.

Was it my client? Again, no. He wasn't trying to provoke me; he was simply sharing a story he'd heard.

The problem wasn't the story itself—it was my reaction to it. Why did this news shake me so much?

I turned to an exercise my Inner Wizard taught me: viewing the situation in 3D. This means stepping back and looking at the issue from a higher perspective, like a bird's-eye view. When you do this, you strip away the surface-level noise and get closer to the truth.

And the truth? The real villain here was the media.

The media thrives on sensationalism. Their goal isn't to inform or unite; it's to divide, provoke, and get clicks. The phrase *"if it bleeds, it leads"* has been their playbook for decades. They don't care about truth or nuance—they care about attention.

I wanted to confirm the story, so I did a quick Google search: *"schools putting litter boxes in bathrooms."*

Every result on the first page included words like "hoax," "rumor," or "false." The story wasn't even true. Apparently, it all started with a Nebraska state senator who made this wild claim in December 2022. From there, it spread like wildfire, with news outlets picking it up without verifying a single detail.

This wasn't just misinformation—it was a deliberate tactic to provoke outrage, judgment, and division. And it worked. My client was rattled enough to share it with me, which in turn got me worked up. The media knew exactly how to trigger emotions, ensuring the story would spread further.

We all know someone who's completely brainwashed by the news they consume. It doesn't matter whether they're glued to CNN or Fox News—both create silos that cater to reactionary emotions, feeding viewers a surface layer of sensationalism. For some, it's not just a bad habit—it's an addiction.

As with any addiction—be it alcohol, cigarettes, gambling, food, or yes, even the news—the loser is always the addict.

Here's the thing: it's not just the news they're addicted to. It's the emotions the news triggers. They're hooked on the cycle of judgment, blame, and self-righteous anger. They complain. They justify their outrage. They feed their narratives of "us versus them." Maybe they even love to argue, and the news gives them the perfect ammunition to start fights.

But what are they really doing? They're fueling their misery.

News outlets know exactly what they're doing, too. They're not interested in educating or uniting people. They feed their viewers a steady diet of outrage and fear because they know it keeps them coming back for more. It's a toxic loop, and just like any other addiction, it's tough to break free from.

Once I viewed this situation in 3D, everything clicked. The media's goal isn't unity—it's stoking judgment and hate to keep people distracted and compliant.

And that's not the legacy I want to pass on to my children.

Even though the story was a hoax, it forced me to reevaluate my values. Would I be okay with litter boxes in schools? No. Do I think kids should identify as animals? Also no. But do I think kids genuinely believe they're animals? Of course not—they're kids. They're playful, imaginative, and testing boundaries like every generation before them.

The real issue wasn't the kids. It was my reaction.

Spurred to Action

This roller coaster of an event moved me in a way I hadn't expected—it pushed me to act. The furry hoax wasn't just a bizarre rumor; it was a reminder of how easily we can get caught up in surface-level noise.

We live in a world where most of us skim the surface layer, reacting to headlines and half-truths. But the surface only gives you chaos. If you want truth, peace, and understanding, you have to dig deeper. You need to see beyond what's obvious.

We need to go deeper to rise above. (How's that for an oxymoron?)

I hated how much power that story had over me. It dictated my emotions, consumed my energy, and even made me angry—for something that wasn't even true. For that brief moment, I had given away all control to the media. I don't want anyone—let alone a misleading news story—to have that much control over me. What kind of example would that set for my kids?

Once I stepped back and looked at the situation in 3D, I saw the truth. I identified the real bad guy, and suddenly my confusion, judgment, and anger disappeared like steam from a hot shower. Because I had learned how to master my emotions, I regained control. I understood what was happening, and it no longer affected me.

I was free from media manipulation.

But this wasn't just about me. It was also about my family. I felt compelled to share this experience with my wife and how we could approach teaching our kids. I didn't want my children to get stuck in 2D thinking, judging others or allowing hate to creep into their hearts simply because they didn't see the bigger picture.

That false furry story was more than just fake news; it became the spark for deeper reflection. It inspired me to ask myself: *What do I stand for? What values do I hold?*

And, more importantly: *What values am I teaching my kids?*

Meet Your Inner King

Every dad has an Inner King. He's the part of you that wants to lead, to provide, and to protect your family. He is the steady hand on the wheel, steering your household toward purpose and stability. The Inner King is the ruler of your castle, the architect of your family's foundation, and the protector of what matters most.

This archetype is about more than just making decisions or providing financially—it's about creating a legacy. Your Inner King thrives on purpose and responsibility. He is driven by values that shape the environment of your home, guide your actions, and set the tone for how your family moves through the world.

When your Inner King is at his best, he's a leader who acts with clarity and intention. He sees the bigger picture and takes steps to align his family with a shared vision. He's the one who introduces family traditions, defines what is important, and leads by example. Whether it's teaching your kids the importance of kindness or helping your spouse feel supported, the Inner King is always looking to build a stronger, healthier, and more connected family.

But the King doesn't operate alone—he needs tools to reign effectively. One of the most powerful tools in his arsenal is a clear set of values. Values are the compass your Inner King uses to navigate the challenges of parenting, relationships, and life. They provide the framework for how you make decisions, solve problems, and respond to the inevitable curveballs life throws your way.

For example, think about a moment when your child was having a tough day. Maybe they came home from school upset because they didn't make the basketball team. The Inner King doesn't dismiss their feelings or try to solve the problem right away. Instead, he listens. He validates their emotions and gently reminds them that setbacks are part of growth. He might even share a personal story of a time he faced rejection and how it ultimately shaped him for the better.

Or imagine a situation at work where a team member made a mistake that cost the company money. The Inner King doesn't rush to anger or blame. Instead, he uses the moment as a teaching opportunity. He leads with grace, reminding his team that mistakes happen and focusing on what can be learned to prevent it from happening again.

The Inner King isn't about perfection; he's about progress. He's about showing up consistently, even when it's hard. He's about prioritizing what truly matters and finding ways to elevate those around him. He creates stability, but he's not afraid to adapt when circumstances change.

Every dad has this Inner King within him—ready to lead, ready to provide, and ready to protect. The challenge is tapping into that kingly energy intentionally. Too often, we get caught up in the chaos of life, reacting instead of leading. The Inner King reminds us to pause, reflect, and make choices that align with our higher purpose.

This chapter will guide you through one of the most important tools your Inner King can use: defining your family values. Because when your Inner King reigns with clarity and purpose, your family thrives.

Jet Fuel: The Power of Values

Every family has values—whether they've been written down or not. If I asked you to name yours, you could probably rattle off a few. But here's the real test: Would the rest of your family name the same ones?

That's where the magic happens—or doesn't. While every family has values, not every family makes them explicit. And when values aren't clear or shared, confusion can creep in. How can a family truly live its values if no one is on the same page?

Values are like a compass for your household. They guide how you treat one another, how you respond to challenges, and how you make decisions. Without them, you're sailing without a map.

When I was growing up, my parents never sat me down to talk about values. They were implied—and I picked them up here and there through actions or expectations—but they were never explicitly discussed or written down. Back then, that approach worked. Life was simpler. The media didn't have a stranglehold on our lives. News came from a few channels, and you had to intentionally tune in to hear it.

Today, it's a whole new ball game. The media is relentless, infiltrating every corner of our lives. News, gossip, and controversy are just a swipe away, 24/7. Smartphones and social media have amplified the noise, turning every story into a distraction designed to grab our attention and pull us off course.

In this world of constant noise and distractions, the need for clear, intentional values has never been greater. As dads, it's up to us to lead the charge. If we don't teach our kids our values, the world will gladly teach them something else.

That's why, in July 2023, I sat down and officially wrote out my family's values. This wasn't a list I imposed on my family like some sort of kingly decree. It was the result of thoughtful conversations about what we already care about, how we live, and what we'd like to emphasize more.

The process was an opportunity to connect with my family in a deeper way. It became a shared vision—a compass we could all use to navigate life together.

What does your family stand for?

If you don't have a clear answer yet, don't worry. The goal isn't perfection. It's about starting the conversation. Begin by reflecting on your life today. What do you value most? What behaviors do you already encourage in your family? Once you have a rough idea, share it with your spouse and kids. Let them contribute their thoughts.

Values aren't meant to be dictated; they're meant to be discovered together.

And if you're feeling unsure or overwhelmed, don't stress. You don't have to do this alone. In the next section, I'll walk you through a simple exercise to help you uncover your family's unique set of values. Together, we'll create a guiding compass to lead your family forward.

Find Your Values

Finding your values is a fun and transformative exercise. It's an opportunity to reflect on what truly matters to you, your family, or your team. The process is simple but powerful, and I'll walk you through how I've done it personally, with my family, and at work.

Personal Values

Before we dive into family or team values, let's start with you. Identifying your personal values is essential because they serve as the foundation for how you navigate life. They influence every decision you make, whether consciously or subconsciously. Your personal values act as a compass, guiding your actions, reactions, and priorities.

When you're clear on your personal values, you can live with greater authenticity and purpose. It's easier to make decisions because you have a built-in framework for what matters most. Without them, you might find yourself drifting, making choices based on convenience or external pressures rather than alignment with who you truly are.

For example, if one of your values is integrity, you'll naturally prioritize honesty and trustworthiness, even when it's inconvenient. If another is health, you'll be more inclined to make decisions that support your well-being, like eating nutritious meals or prioritizing exercise.

Personal values are also the starting point for creating a ripple effect. When you know your values, you can lead by example. Your kids, spouse, or team will see those values in action, and it'll inspire them to reflect on their own.

This isn't just about being a good parent, partner, or leader—it's about being the best version of yourself. And that starts with clarity.

So, how do you figure out your values?

Start by grabbing a list of values. You can find plenty online, or you can use the one provided in these pages.

Take some time to review the words on the list. Highlight or circle fifteen to twenty that resonate with you. Ask yourself:

- What do I value most in myself?
- What do I admire in others?
- What qualities light me up?

Take a moment right now to highlight or circle. Once you've highlighted fifteen to twenty, narrow them down to your top five to ten. Then, rank those in order of importance. This step is crucial because ranking forces you to make intentional choices.

Go ahead. I'll wait.

Here's a simple way to prioritize: compare two values and ask, *Which is more important to me right now?* For example, is curiosity more important than love? If you choose love, it outranks curiosity. Repeat this process with the rest of your values until you have a ranked list.

- Authenticity
- Achievement
- Adventure
- Attraction
- Authority
- Autonomy
- Balance
- Being My Best
- Boldness
- Compassion
- Challenge
- Citizenship
- Community
- Competency
- Contribution
- Courage
- Creativity
- Curiosity
- Determination
- Discipline
- Discovery
- Empathetic
- Fairness
- Faith
- Fame
- Freedom
- Friendships
- Fun
- Generosity
- Growth
- Gratitude
- Happiness
- Health
- Honesty
- Humor
- Influence
- Innovative
- Inspirational
- Intelligence
- Inner Harmony
- Integrity
- Joyfulness
- Justice
- Kindness
- Knowledge
- Leadership
- Learning
- Love
- Loyalty
- Meaningful Work
- Meritocracy
- Openness
- Optimism
- Passion
- Peace
- Playful
- Pleasure
- Poise
- Popularity
- Progress
- Recognition
- Religion
- Reputation
- Respect
- Responsibility
- Security
- Self-Respect
- Service
- Sharing
- Spirituality
- Stability
- Status
- Strength
- Success
- Sympathetic
- Transparency
- Trustworthiness
- Uniqueness
- Wealth
- Wisdom

My personal values have evolved over time, but as of writing this book, here's my current list in order:

1. Love
2. Gratefulness
3. Grit
4. Intelligence
5. Health & Wellness
6. Success & Achievement

Success & Achievement used to be my number one—driven by a little boy shoved into trash cans, desperate to prove his worth. This value came above all else, including my wife and family. I worked hard to succeed, and everyone around me knew it.

Today, it's still part of me, but it's no longer in the driver's seat. I've redefined success, moving away from money and status toward fulfillment and balance.

Love is intentionally my number-one value now. It's the core of who we are as humans, and it's what we're wired for. Looking back, all I ever wanted was to feel loved and accepted. And let's be real—*what's more important for a dad than love?*

Pro tip: Check your values every year or two. Life changes, and so do your priorities. Keep your values updated to reflect the person you're becoming.

Family Values

Creating family values is similar to creating personal ones, but this time, it's a team effort. In July 2023, I officially wrote down eight principles for my family. These weren't mandates I forced on my wife and kids. Instead, we reflected together on what we care about and what we'd like to emphasize more.

Here's what we landed on:

1. Kindness
2. Freedom

3.   Growth
4.   Meritocracy
5.   Gratitude
6.   Generosity
7.   Health
8.   Community

These values serve as our family's compass. They guide how we interact with one another and the world around us. I encourage you to do the same. Talk with your family about what matters most to you collectively. Let everyone contribute. When everyone has a say, they're more likely to embrace the values as a team.

Workplace Values

Establishing values at work is a game-changer. Values streamline decision-making, empower teams, and reduce unnecessary questions and approvals. When everyone aligns with shared values, operations flow more smoothly, and the work culture thrives.

At my firm, we did this as a team. I distributed a list of values to my management team and asked them, *What do we care most about here?*

I divided them into smaller groups and tasked each group with narrowing the list to four or five values. Then, we came together to combine the results. Using stars to highlight overlaps, we identified our top contenders. After some discussion, we finalized our top five:

1.   Caring & Community
2.   Outstanding Service

3. Growth & Innovation
4. Gratitude
5. Fun, Fulfillment, & Happiness

From this, our mission statement was born: *"We Excel Because We Care."*

This collaborative process gave everyone ownership over the values. It wasn't about me dictating what mattered—it was about us deciding together. This sense of ownership fostered buy-in from the team and created a culture of independent, empowered decision-making.

Here's a real example: One of our managers recently sent flowers to a client who had lost her dog. She didn't ask for permission; she didn't need to. She knew it aligned with our values, so she acted.

If you're not in a position to lead this discussion at your workplace, don't hesitate to suggest it to your supervisor or manager. A values-driven workplace benefits everyone.

Once you've identified your personal, family, or workplace values, the next step is to codify them.

Codify Your Values

One-word values are a great foundation, but turning those words into actionable principles takes them to the next level. Codifying your values means clearly defining them in a systematic way so that they're tangible, actionable, and easy to apply in everyday life. By codifying values, you ensure that their meaning is consistent, their application is intentional, and their impact is far-reaching.

Why codify? Because values without clarity are like a map with no directions—they give you a sense of where to go but no real guidance on how to get there. Codified values act as your compass, shaping your habits and helping you establish the rules that govern your family or team dynamics.

In other words, codifying your values makes them tangible.

Calling back to the Triangle of Beliefs from the previous chapter, codifying your values helps establish meaning, rules, and habits. Codifying values helps ensure members of your family or your team are on the same page when it comes to the *meaning* behind each word. The unit can then create a loose set of *rules* for each one. And the more tangible, the better the habits.

My Family's Codified Values

For the purpose of this chapter, here's how we turned our family's values into clear, actionable principles that guide our decisions and interactions:

1. **Kindness = The Golden Rule**

    You've probably heard this since kindergarten: *Treat others the way you want to be treated.* It's simple, timeless, and universal, showing up in various cultures and religions worldwide. Even my daughters' Girl Scout troop recites it regularly.

The Golden Rule is kindness distilled. It's about empathy, respect, and creating harmony in relationships. While the hoax story about furries inspired me to write down our family's values, I realized kindness had to come first. Why? Because you can practice kindness even in the most constrained circumstances.

Think of Nelson Mandela, who spent twenty-five years in prison preparing himself to lead South Africa with dignity and grace. Kindness isn't dependent on freedom—it's a choice.

2. Freedom = Protect and respect freedom of beliefs and speech

Freedom is essential, but it comes with responsibility. In our family, we believe in respecting people's right to their beliefs, even if we disagree. That doesn't mean freedom is limitless— freedom of speech, for example, doesn't grant the right to scream *fire* in a crowded theater.

True freedom thrives within boundaries that protect everyone's rights.

3. Growth = Growth mindset

Life deals everyone a hand, and most of it is out of our control. But how you play your cards—that's where growth comes in. A growth mindset is about embracing challenges, learning from failures, and striving for progress.

Tony Robbins famously says, *"Progress equals happiness."* We're dynamic beings; we evolve whether we want to or not. The key is to grow intentionally.

This concept resonated with my daughters immediately. "Mr. Zakudo is gonna love this!" they exclaimed. Brad Zakudo is their principal, and his school emphasizes a growth mindset. Hearing their excitement made me proud to see this principle being taught at such a young age.

4. **Meritocracy = Fairness**

Meritocracy means being rewarded for your efforts and achievements. It's about fairness—getting what you earn, not what you're entitled to.

Life isn't always fair, but the systems we operate within should strive to be. I've been fortunate to work in a field that values merit over nepotism. In accounting, you start at the bottom, prove your skills, and earn your way up. It's a shame this isn't the norm in every industry.

In our family, meritocracy teaches my kids that rewards come from hard work, not entitlement. Life doesn't owe us anything just because we exist—we earn our way through grit and perseverance.

5. **Gratitude = Attitude of gratitude and your mindset matters**

Gratitude is transformative. It reframes challenges, highlights blessings, and keeps you grounded. It's not about denying the tough parts of life but finding the good in the mess.

Like any habit, gratitude takes practice. Start small:

I'm grateful for the sun shining today.

I'm grateful for a warm cup of coffee.

The more you practice, the more natural it becomes. Gratitude isn't just about saying thank you—it's about living with an appreciation for life's gifts, big and small.

6. **Generosity = Give more than you take**

Generosity isn't just about money—it's a mindset. Be generous with your time, your kindness, and your talents.

When I was growing up, people often commented on my generosity. One Christmas when I was ten, I used my own money to buy my sister a gumball machine. I even filled it with gumballs so she could use it right away. Seeing her joy was unforgettable and taught me that giving is its own reward.

Generosity has a ripple effect. The more you give, the more you receive—often in unexpected and beautiful ways.

7. **Health = Stop and smell the roses, eat an apple a day, and look up at the stars in amazement**

Health is the ultimate foundation for everything. Without it, even the best of intentions—these principles included—become incredibly hard to live out.

Each of these sayings touches on mind, body, and spirit.

Sure, they're clichés, but they endure for a reason. Let's break them down:

Stop and smell the roses: At first glance, this reminds us to slow down, step out of life's endless hustle, and find joy in the small, beautiful moments. But it's more than that. If you're stopping to smell the roses, you're probably outside, and that means you're moving, even if it's just a little. This simple act nurtures both your mind and your body.

Eat an apple a day: You've likely heard the full version, "An apple a day keeps the doctor away." It's about the importance of eating healthy to maintain physical well-being and avoid unnecessary visits to the doctor. But look deeper: an apple represents whole, unprocessed food, grown from the earth, with no ingredient list needed. Eating more whole foods and cutting down on processed ones is key to a healthier body and mind.

Look up at the stars in amazement: The stars are always there, appearing like clockwork every night, but how often do we pause to notice? Staring up at the vastness of the universe has a way of putting life into perspective. With an estimated 100–200 million stars in our galaxy alone, and billions of galaxies beyond that, it's humbling to think about our place in such an enormous, awe-inspiring cosmos. Taking a moment to connect with something so much greater than ourselves nourishes the spirit and reminds us to slow down and be present.

Together, these phrases are reminders to care for your health in every sense—mind, body, and spirit—so you can fully embrace life and all it offers. After all, as the saying goes, *"Health is wealth."*

8. **Community = Help others who are helping themselves**

Helping others is an important value, but it comes with a critical distinction: help those *who are willing to help themselves.* Notice this codified value doesn't stop at just "helping others." Although noble, it's hard to help people who don't want to be helped. But when someone is actively trying to improve their situation, that's where we can step in.

This principle avoids the trap of preachiness—no one likes being lectured. Instead, it's about recognizing when someone is putting in effort and meeting them where they are. It creates a mutually beneficial exchange. By helping someone who's already on their journey, you're not only supporting their growth, but you're also engaging in a fulfilling act for yourself.

When we teach or assist others who are striving to help themselves, they gain knowledge, tools, or encouragement to keep going, and we feel good knowing we've made a positive impact.

It's the ultimate win-win.

Leaving Your Legacy

Every one of us has a desire to feel important, valued, and unique. That's your Inner King, stepping forward to lead your family with purpose and intention. As kings of our castles, we have a responsibility to guide our families, and the best way to do that is by establishing and living by our values. These values are more than just words—they're the foundation for how we interact, make decisions, and respond to life's challenges.

And here's the beauty of it: it's never too early—or too late—to start. Whether your kids are toddlers or teenagers, introducing and living out family values is one of the most meaningful contributions you can make as a dad. Writing them down, talking about them daily, and embodying them creates a legacy that extends far beyond material possessions or financial support.

For me, codifying our family values was a way to connect more deeply with my daughters and contribute to our home in a way that went beyond providing a paycheck. It became a chance to get involved and bring something deeply worthwhile to the table. And let me tell you—the return has been priceless.

These days, our values come up in conversation naturally. My girls know them by heart, and they share them proudly, whether it's over dinner with guests or as a casual mention during a family outing. The impact doesn't stop at home, either. I've shared our values with my clients and even with the board of an organization I joined to support children in need. The ripple effect is undeniable.

If you're unsure where to begin, don't overcomplicate it. Use my family's list as a starting point, or create your own through thoughtful conversations with your spouse and kids. Once you identify your values, commit to them. Feel them. Live them. Breathe them. Let your actions reflect them every day because your kids are always watching—even more than they're listening.

So, what's the reward for living your values? Certainty, clarity, and unity in a world that often feels chaotic. It's a tool for creating an environment where your family can thrive. When life throws challenges your way, your values will act as a shield against negativity and confusion. Rocks might be thrown, but they'll bounce off—because your family will stand strong in its identity.

As dads, our greatest legacy isn't the money we leave behind but the values we pass on to our children. These values will guide them long after we're gone, shaping how they approach the world and the families they'll create one day.

When your family lives and breathes its values, your household transforms into a kingdom—a place of love, connection, and resilience. And you? You'll feel like the king you were always meant to be.

But even kings can grow too comfortable on their thrones. I realized that my Inner King had given me a sense of stability and direction, but I needed something more. I felt the call to push myself out of my comfort zone and invite a different part of me to step forward.

That's when I turned to my Inner Jester—and that's exactly where we'll go in the next chapter.

CHAPTER 4

Your Inner Jester: Overcoming Limiting Beliefs

"What we fear doing most is usually what we most need to do."
—Tim Ferris

COMFORT CAN FEEL GOOD—UNTIL IT DOESN'T.

Too much comfort can leave you feeling stagnant, stuck in a rut, or just plain bored. That's exactly where I found myself, so I decided to shake things up and intentionally step into unfamiliar territory. My goal was to try new things, challenge myself, and see what happened.

I chose three completely different endeavors to tackle: ice skating, bodybuilding, and writing a book.

First on the list: ice skating. My daughters are incredibly skilled figure skaters, and I thought learning the sport would be a fun way to connect with them while trying something new. It seemed like a win-win.

Ten lessons later, I could make my way across the ice without falling, which I considered a major victory. I was ready to skate with my girls. The problem? At twelve and fourteen, they weren't exactly eager to hit the ice with Dad. Imagine that! (Feel free to laugh here. I did!)

With no one to skate with and no real passion for the sport, I decided to move on. Ice skating was fine, but it didn't light me up or feel meaningful.

Strike one—but hey, at least I tried.

Next, I turned to the gym. Health is one of my core values, and I'd always been intrigued by the idea of achieving six-pack abs. It seemed like a worthy goal, so I committed to more intense workouts and dialing in my diet.

But as the weeks went by, I realized my motivation was entirely self-serving. Vanity wasn't enough to sustain me, and the goal quickly lost its appeal. I wanted to focus on something bigger than just looking good.

Strike two.

That's when I decided to take on something completely different: writing a book.

And let me tell you, the idea terrified me.

I'm a numbers guy. Words are not exactly my thing. How the hell was I supposed to write a book—especially one that had nothing to do with accounting or numbers? Growing up, I wasn't much of a reader, and my writing skills were mediocre at best. (Full disclosure: I cheated my way through one of my high school English classes.)

But that's exactly why I knew I had to do it.

Taking on the challenge of writing a book stretched me far beyond my comfort zone. It was about proving to myself that I could tackle something I'd never done before. It was an opportunity to grow, to set a vision for myself, and to see it through.

I started by enrolling in a writing course in Nashville, Tennessee, led by authors Allison Fallon and Donald Miller. Don, who's also the CEO of StoryBrand, was a dynamic and inspiring teacher. Out of thirty participants, I was one of only three men in the room—a fact that struck me. It made me realize just how many women are out there, eager to share their stories. Husbands, take note: listen to your wives!

The course, called *Write Your Story*, helped me solidify my decision to write this book.

"I didn't come this far to only get this far," I told myself.

Writing wasn't just a test of my skills—it was a test of my courage. Sharing my struggles with alcohol and the impact it had on my marriage wasn't easy. Writing about my past meant exposing myself to public judgment, which was intimidating.

And on top of that, I worried people might assume I wrote this book to seek attention or feed my ego—neither of which is true. If anything, those assumptions horrified me.

But that's what made this challenge so worthwhile. It forced me to confront my fears, get uncomfortable, and grow in ways I didn't expect.

It's easy to stay in our comfort zones, but that's not where growth happens. Trying these three new things—whether I succeeded or not—reminded me that stepping into the unknown is where life gets interesting.

Meet Your Inner Jester

Life can feel heavy when we take ourselves too seriously. The responsibilities of family, work, and our own ambitions can weigh us down, leaving little room for lightness, curiosity, or play.

Enter your Inner Jester—the playful, daring archetype that lives within all of us. The Jester is your guide to curiosity and transformation. It's the part of you that says, "Why not?" when you're stuck in a rut. When your Inner King is too busy sitting on his throne, managing rules and expectations, your Inner Jester is the one tugging at his cape, asking, "Let's do something new! What if we did this?"

The Inner Jester thrives on variety, humor, and adventure. It nudges you to step outside the boundaries of your comfort zone, daring you to explore new possibilities. Unlike your King, who values structure and stability, the Jester embraces uncertainty and sees failure not as a dead end but as a stepping stone to growth.

Your Inner Jester is the spark of curiosity that leads you to try something new. It's the courage to take on a passion project that scares the hell out of you. And perhaps most importantly, it's the humility to laugh at yourself when things don't go as planned.

This archetype brings an essential energy to your life: playfulness. When life feels monotonous, the Jester asks, "What's something different we can try?" It's not about being reckless—it's about being bold enough to embrace variety, to shake things up, and to look for the humor in your missteps.

Humor, after all, is a powerful bridge. It connects you to others and softens the edges of failure. It makes daunting tasks feel lighter and helps you reframe challenges as opportunities. Your Jester isn't here to undermine the King's rule—it's here to remind him that growth and transformation often come through trial, error, and a good laugh.

How does your Inner Jester show up? Your Jester manifests in countless ways:

- It's the impulse to pick up a guitar you've never played and strum your way through a song, off-key and all.
- It's the whim to sign up for a half-marathon when you've barely jogged a mile.
- It's the voice in your head that dares you to take on a passion project, even though you have no idea where to begin.
- It's the grace to laugh at yourself when you trip over your own shoelaces, both metaphorically and literally.

The Jester isn't about perfect outcomes—it's about the process, the journey, and the joy of trying. When you embrace this playful side of yourself, you create room for transformation.

Jet Fuel for Your Inner Jester

How do you awaken your Inner Jester, that part of you that thrives on variety, boldness, and a dash of playful rebellion? Start by asking yourself one powerful question: *How can I step outside my comfort zone?*

Imagine life as a treasure hunt, where the most valuable rewards lie just beyond the edges of your current reality. To uncover these treasures, you'll need to take a leap of faith, embrace the unknown, and dare to try something new—even if it feels a little daunting.

Begin small. Ask yourself:

- Is there a hobby you've always been curious about but haven't yet explored?
- Is there a creative outlet calling your name?
- Is there a physical goal you've dreamed about but convinced yourself you're not ready for?

Write down a list of three to five things you've always wanted to try. Maybe it's something ambitious, like writing a book, or something lighthearted, like learning to salsa dance. Maybe it's rekindling an old hobby you loved as a child or testing your limits at the gym.

Whatever it is, let your Jester guide you. Choose something that piques your interest and lies just outside your current expertise. Your Jester craves novelty and playfulness, but it's also strategic—it knows growth comes from trying and failing, not from playing it safe.

Take a moment right now to pause, grab a pen and paper, and write down your top three to five ideas. There's something about putting pen to paper that solidifies your thoughts and brings your intentions to life.

What was your childhood dream? Maybe it was becoming an astronaut, a rock star, or even the president. This is your chance to reconnect with that spark of wonder. Somewhere along the way, in the process of growing up, many of us muted the limitless imagination we had as kids.

Your Inner Jester is here to reignite that sense of possibility, to remind you what it feels like to dream big without constraints. So, give yourself permission to dream like a kid again. Take a few moments, let your imagination run wild, and write down the dreams that light you up—no matter how outlandish or impossible they may seem. This exercise isn't about practicality; it's about rediscovering the joy and excitement of dreaming without limits.

If you're having a hard go, don't worry. We'll explore how to awaken your Inner Jester by tackling three essential jet fuel options for growth: overcoming limiting beliefs, embracing the fear of failure, and learning to laugh at yourself.

These practices help you step outside your comfort zone, confront the barriers that hold you back, and find humor in the journey—all while nurturing the playful, daring spirit that fuels transformation.

By embracing these lessons, you'll not only invite your Inner Jester to the forefront but also unlock a path to a more vibrant, adventurous, and fulfilling life.

Overcoming Limiting Beliefs

The Inner Jester thrives on boldness, creativity, and the willingness to embrace the unknown. But for this playful archetype to truly shine, we must first confront the invisible chains that hold us back—our limiting beliefs. These beliefs act like brick walls in our minds, blocking our path to the uncharted territories where growth, joy, and transformation reside. They're the false stories we tell ourselves: *"I'm not good enough," "I can't do this," "That's not for me."*

These beliefs often stem from our upbringing, societal programming, or past experiences. Over time, they settle into the background, subtly shaping how we live, the risks we take, and the goals we pursue.

Recognizing these beliefs is the first step to dismantling them. Think about it: What belief is holding you back right now? What's stopping you from pursuing the life you want?

To truly embrace your Inner Jester, you must be willing to step into the unknown and take bold, playful action. Here are a few ideas:

1. **Get Comfortable with the Uncomfortable**

    Breaking free from limiting beliefs means embracing discomfort. It's not about recklessly diving into fear—it's about stepping intentionally into situations that challenge your boundaries.

The truth is, our subconscious craves safety, but safety doesn't lead to growth. Your Inner Jester knows this and dares you to try anyway.

This isn't about conquering surface-level phobias. It's deeper. It's about facing the fears your psyche guards fiercely—the fears of rejection, failure, or inadequacy. Your Jester reminds you that growth and transformation only happen when you lean into these discomforts.

2. **Revisit Your Unfulfilled Desires**

What have you always wanted to do but told yourself you couldn't? Maybe you've avoided pursuing a dream, convincing yourself the timing isn't right or that you're not talented enough. Your Jester knows better. If anything were possible, what would you choose to do?

Would you start that business you've always dreamed of? Perform music at a local coffee shop? Move abroad? Hike the Grand Canyon? Write the book you've been talking about for years?

Your unfulfilled desires often point directly to your limiting beliefs. They reveal the walls you've built and show you where to start knocking them down.

3. **Think of Your Death**

Imagine for a moment that tomorrow is your last day. What regrets would weigh on you? Would you wish you'd taken more chances, followed your passions, or spent more time on what truly mattered?

Yes, this is an unsettling question—but it's a powerful one. It shines a light on the gap between where you are and where you want to be. And it reminds you that the only way to close that gap is to embrace the uncomfortable, to face your fears, and to do the things that scare you.

Growth is life's ultimate fuel. It's the juice that energizes your Inner Jester and keeps you moving forward. As Tony Robbins says, "If you're not growing, you're dying."

Your Jester doesn't shy away from growth—it craves it. It's the archetype that nudges you toward new adventures, dares you to dream bigger, and reminds you to laugh at the stumbles along the way.

Your Inner Jester is here to help you rewrite those false stories and push past your comfort zone. It's not about throwing caution to the wind; it's about summoning the courage to ask yourself: *What if?* And then taking the next step, no matter how small.

Because when you start challenging your limiting beliefs, you unlock a life that's richer, fuller, and infinitely more rewarding.

Embracing the Fear of Failure

In 1976, Steve Jobs and Steve Wozniak, the dynamic duo behind

Apple Computer, set out on a revolutionary journey that would change the world. Yet, there was an unexpected truth: Steve Jobs, the visionary behind the brand, couldn't even balance a checkbook at the time. When Jobs proposed they co-found a computer company, Wozniak responded with a perspective that transcended mere success or failure. "Even if we fail," he said, "whatever we do will be a win. At least I'll have the experience of going into business with a friend."

That mindset—the embrace of adventure over outcome—is a lesson in courage. Failure, like an uninvited guest, sneaks into our lives, convincing us to avoid risks, to stay comfortable. But the sooner we accept failure as part of the process, the sooner we can laugh at ourselves and share our missteps. For Wozniak, failure wasn't something to fear; it was just another stepping stone. Had Apple collapsed, it would have been a story to recount with humor—a riveting chapter, not the end of the book.

Of course, we know how that story turned out. It wasn't a failure. But their willingness to face the possibility of failure was what made it all possible.

Fear of failure is one of the greatest obstacles to pursuing our dreams. Where does it come from? Often, it's woven into our conditioning—the little whispers that say, *"I can't do this," "I don't have time," "I can't afford it."* These beliefs shackle us, keeping us from chasing the desires that stir our souls.

It's time to challenge those whispers. What would you do if failure wasn't a factor? If money, time, or resources weren't an issue, what dream would you pursue? These questions strip away the layers of practicality, revealing the longings we bury beneath excuses and fears.

For me, these questions have been transformative. I love my job, and I find deep fulfillment in it, but I've always felt a calling for something more—something uncharted. This book, for example, is part of that puzzle. Most accountants settle into their careers until retirement, but for me, staying in this field until I'm seventy would mean I failed. Not at accounting, but at confronting my fears and answering that inner call.

Failure isn't the enemy. Stagnation is. And the real loss is never trying.

Fear of failure is the antithesis of your Inner Jester. The Jester thrives on curiosity, exploration, and playfulness—the very things that fear tries to suppress. It's the Jester's voice that dares you to leap into the unknown, to treat failure as part of the dance rather than the end of the song. By embracing your Inner Jester, you reframe failure not as a threat but as a natural, even humorous, stepping stone toward growth. Your Jester reminds you that life is too short to take yourself so seriously and too precious to let fear keep you from experiencing all it has to offer.

So, listen to that playful voice, take the leap, and trust that the story—even with its stumbles—will be worth telling.

Learning to Laugh at Yourself

Laughter is the jet fuel your Inner Jester craves. When we stumble or when plans unravel, we're handed a choice: to cringe in embarrassment or chuckle in delight. Failure doesn't have to be the end of the road—it can be a stepping stone, an opportunity to smile at our imperfections and remind ourselves that we're all just humans, figuring it out as we go. Each misstep becomes a vibrant brushstroke on the canvas of our lives—a quirky tale to share, a lesson learned, or a memory that adds color to our story.

Writing this book has been my personal prescription for embracing discomfort. It forced me to tap into my Inner Jester, finding humor in the chaos and wisdom in the whimsical. It taught me to let go of the fear of looking foolish and instead lean into the experience, knowing that growth is often hidden in the absurdity.

What do we really stand to lose by trying? Like Steve Jobs and Steve Wozniak asking themselves this very question, the answer is almost always: nothing. But what might we gain? Everything. Your Inner Jester knows that the rewards of trying far outweigh the risks of failing.

Life is a circus, and we're all performers in this grand spectacle. The sooner you embrace your Inner Jester, the sooner you'll realize it's okay to trip over your own shoelaces, laugh at your fumbles, and keep moving forward. Don't let the fear of failure rob you of the joy of the journey.

When you dance with failure—when you laugh with it—you discover your most authentic self. So, embrace the Jester within, find the humor in your stumbles, and live boldly.

Because, let's be honest: the best stories come from missteps anyway.

Not a Straight Line

Life is not a straight line—it's a dance, a journey filled with unexpected twists, turns, and, yes, plenty of stumbles. But here's the secret: those missteps are where the magic happens. Your Inner Jester knows this truth. It thrives in the chaos, laughs in the face of failure, and urges you to embrace life with curiosity and boldness.

Over the course of this chapter, we've explored jet fuel options for awakening your Inner Jester—overcoming limiting beliefs, embracing failure as a stepping stone, and finding freedom in humor. These aren't just practices; they're invitations to step outside your comfort zone, rewrite the false stories you've told yourself, and unlock the vibrant, adventurous life you're meant to lead.

Your Jester isn't here to undermine the structure of your Inner King or Warrior—it's here to complement them. It reminds you that growth doesn't come from perfection but from playfulness. That success isn't measured by the absence of failure but by the willingness to keep trying. That the ability to laugh at yourself isn't a weakness but a strength—a mark of resilience and humility.

When you embrace your Inner Jester, you grant yourself permission to live more fully. You stop fearing failure and start seeing it as part of the process. You stop taking yourself so seriously and start finding joy in the journey.

So, what are you waiting for? Let your Jester take the lead. Try something new, laugh at the inevitable missteps, and celebrate the stories you'll collect along the way. Because life isn't about avoiding mistakes—it's about living boldly, growing relentlessly, and finding joy in the adventure.

And when you do, you'll discover that the greatest gift your Inner Jester offers isn't just variety or humor—it's the freedom to be unapologetically, gloriously, authentically you.

Conclusion

AT THE HEART OF THIS BOOK LIES A SIMPLE TRUTH: THE TOOLS YOU need to lead an intentional, meaningful life are already within you. Your Inner Warrior, Wizard, King, and Jester are not abstract ideas—they're distinct parts of you, waiting to be activated and harmonized. These archetypes are unique to this framework and represent the ways we can rise to meet life's challenges with purpose and empowerment.

If you're familiar with Tony Robbins's teaching on the six human needs—certainty, variety, significance, love and connection, growth, and contribution—you might wonder how they connect to these archetypes. The short answer? They don't line up exactly, and that's intentional. While Robbins's framework focuses on identifying which needs dominate your life, the archetypes in this book provide a practical guide for cultivating the best parts of yourself to meet those needs in healthy and purposeful ways.

For example, your Warrior may seek certainty by standing strong in the face of adversity, but it also thrives in uncertainty, drawing courage from calculated risks and stepping into the unknown. Your Wizard embodies wisdom and connection but extends beyond love as a feeling to love as action—transforming relationships and emotions into powerful tools for growth. Your King brings significance not through ego but by leading with values, and your Jester finds variety not through escapism but through curiosity, creativity, and joy.

While the archetypes and human needs can complement one another, they're distinct approaches. If you're interested in diving deeper into the six human needs, I encourage you to explore Tony Robbins's work. His insights provide a powerful lens for understanding your motivations and how they shape your life. But the archetypes in this book offer something different: a framework for harmonizing the parts of yourself to live with intention, purpose, and joy.

By embracing your Warrior's courage, your Wizard's wisdom, your King's leadership, and your Jester's playfulness, you can break the cycle of disempowering habits and meet your needs in ways that uplift both you and those around you. Together, these archetypes form a holistic and practical approach to creating a life of fulfillment and impact—starting with the actions you take today.

The Cycle of Transformation

True transformation requires engaging all four archetypes in a dynamic, ongoing cycle. They don't work in isolation—they overlap, support, and enhance one another, creating a living process that keeps you evolving.

For me, this became vividly clear during the Tony Robbins event in 2019 when I experienced the Dickens Process. In that moment, my Inner Warrior stepped forward, forcing me to confront the harsh reality of my inaction. I imagined a future where my daughters stood at my casket, mourning a father who failed to change, who let his bad habits define his legacy. That mental image wasn't just sobering—it was transformational. It showed me the pain of staying the same and the possibility of choosing a different path.

But the Warrior wasn't acting alone. My Wizard helped me reframe that vision into something actionable, showing me how gratitude and clarity could guide my journey. My King reminded me of the values I wanted to embody for my family—courage, integrity, and love—and my Jester whispered, "You can do this. Laugh at your hiccups and enjoy the ride." Each archetype played a role in that breakthrough, creating a ripple effect that continues to shape my life.

This is the power of the archetype cycle. It's not linear; it's a loop. You start with a vision, let it pull you forward, and use each archetype to navigate the challenges along the way. When fear arises, your Warrior steps in with courage. When clarity is needed, your Wizard provides wisdom. When life feels heavy, your Jester lightens the load. And when it's time to stay grounded, your King brings you back to your values. This process repeats endlessly, each round making you stronger, more intentional, and more aligned with your true self.

For much of my life, I operated primarily as a Warrior. I set ambitious goals, pursued them relentlessly, and achieved success by most standards. But success without fulfillment, as Tony Robbins says, is the ultimate failure. I was living proof. The goals kept shifting, and no matter what I accomplished, it never felt like enough. Instead of finding joy, I turned to disempowering habits—drinking, distracting myself, and self-sabotaging the relationships that mattered most.

It wasn't until I stopped drinking in 2019 that I began to embrace the other archetypes. My Wizard taught me how to master my emotions and find fulfillment in the present moment. My King showed me the importance of creating a legacy by documenting my family's values and living them daily. And my Jester reminded me to play, to try new things, and to embrace the discomfort of growth. These archetypes didn't just help me change—they helped me become the father, husband, and man I was meant to be.

And yet, I'm still a work in progress. My Jester challenges me daily to find humor and joy in life's chaos. My Wizard reminds me to slow down and connect with gratitude. My Warrior pushes me to confront fear, and my King grounds me in the values that guide every decision I make. This process is ongoing, and that's what makes it beautiful.

Growth doesn't stop—it evolves.

The Legacy You Leave

As fathers, we hold incredible power to shape the future—not just for ourselves but for our children and generations to come. Our actions, choices, and values ripple outward, creating a legacy that extends far beyond our lifetimes. This isn't about perfection; it's about intention. It's about leading by example and teaching our kids how to live with courage, gratitude, integrity, and joy.

In a world dominated by distractions, algorithms, and divisive narratives, teaching values has never been more important. Schools and society won't fill this void—it's up to us. By defining your family's values and living them every day, you create a compass that keeps everyone rowing in the same direction. Values simplify life. They bring clarity to decisions, unity to relationships, and resilience in the face of challenges.

And it's never too late to start. Whether you're a young father or a grandfather, your influence matters. Even small actions—like writing down your principles, having honest conversations, or simply modeling love and respect—can leave a lasting impact.

Your journey toward creating a legacy of intention, joy, and meaning doesn't have to end here. Everything you need to be successful is already within these pages—the tools, frameworks, and exercises are all here to guide you. But if you're looking for a little accountability or extra guidance, I invite you to join me for a one-day seminar that I host every November. This online seminar is designed to help you dig into the exercises from this book, plan out your next year, and dive deeper into the value chain exercise. It's an opportunity to reflect, connect, and strategize—not just for yourself, but for the legacy you're building for your family. Visit **www.sucklesslaughmore.com** to sign up and secure your spot. With a small fee and a big impact, this seminar is a chance to reinforce the values that will guide your family for generations.

The world may feel chaotic, but you have the power to shape it, starting with your own home. Embrace the four archetypes within you. Let your Warrior lead with courage, your Wizard with wisdom, your King with purpose, and your Jester with playfulness. Together, they form a superior framework for navigating life, ensuring that your children inherit a brighter future.

And lastly: You matter. Your role as a father, a leader, and a human being matters. The legacy you leave isn't just about what you accomplish—it's about who you are and how you live. So, step into the fullness of your archetypes. Create a life of intention, joy, and meaning. Your journey starts now, and the future is yours to build.

It starts with you.

Acknowledgments

Thank you to everyone who has cheered me on throughout this journey—from my incredible parents, Rick and Marianne, to my sisters and their husbands, and my uncles and cousins. Your encouragement has meant the world to me. My gratitude also extends to my work family—Keith, Eve, Ben, Yishai—and to my former colleagues, Michael, Shannon, Marie, and Carl. Your support has been invaluable, and I'm deeply thankful for all of you.

About the Author

Brian Gray is a tax advisor, problem solver, and lifelong learner who believes in finding balance between professional excellence and personal fulfillment. As a partner at Gursey Schneider, he works with high-net-worth individuals, families, and their advisors to design tax-efficient estate plans, maximize wealth-transfer opportunities, and solve complex financial challenges. Known for his collaborative approach, Brian leads a team of skilled professionals who strive to provide sophisticated solutions with a boutique-level personal touch.

A graduate of the University of California, Santa Barbara, Brian holds a Bachelor of Arts degree in Business Economics with a minor in Accounting. He is a member of the California Society of Certified Public Accountants and the American Institute of Certified Public Accountants, and he regularly presents at conferences, including the USC Tax Institute.

When he's not immersed in tax strategy or helping clients achieve their goals, Brian values time with his wife and two daughters in Los Angeles, where they embrace the joys and challenges of family life.

Whether tackling a mountain on a snowboard or unwinding with a great book or documentary, Brian finds inspiration in the balance between work and play.

www.ingramcontent.com/pod-product-compliance
Lightning Source LLC
Chambersburg PA
CBHW051317120626
46547CB00015B/2279